THE FATE
OF MEANING

THE FATE
OF MEANING

▽

Charles Peirce, Structuralism,
and Literature

JOHN K. SHERIFF

PRINCETON UNIVERSITY PRESS
Princeton, New Jersey

Copyright © 1989 by Princeton University Press
Published by Princeton University Press, 41 William Street
Princeton, New Jersey 08540
In the United Kingdom: Princeton University Press,
Guildford, Surrey

Library of Congress Cataloging-in-Publication Data
Sheriff, John K., 1944–
The fate of meaning : Charles Peirce, structuralism, and literature / by
John K. Sheriff.
p.   cm.
Includes index.
ISBN 0-691-06762-7 (alk. paper) ISBN 0-691-01450-7 (phk.)
1. Literature—Philosophy. 2. Hermeneutics. 3. Meaning (Psychology).
4. Peirce, Charles S. (Charles Sanders), 1839–1914—Influence.
5. Semiotics and literature. I. Title. PN81.S43 1989
801'.41—dc19   88-19580
CIP

Publication of this book has been aided by a grant from
the Paul Mellon Fund of Princeton University Press

This book has been composed in Linotron Granjon

Clothbound editions of Princeton University Press books
are printed on acid-free paper, and binding materials are
chosen for strength and durability.
Paperbacks, although satisfactory for personal collections,
are not usually suitable for library rebinding

Printed in the United States of America by
Princeton University Press,
Princeton, New Jersey

FOR ELSIE

CONTENTS

ACKNOWLEDGMENTS

The writing of this book was made possible by a Research Fellowship for College Teachers from the National Endowment for the Humanities and an Andrew Mellow Post-Doctoral Senior Fellowship for Research in Semiotics from Kansas University.

Portions of Chapters 4 and 5 were previously published in my article "Charles S. Peirce and the Semiotics of Literature," in Richard T. DeGeorge, ed., *Semiotic Themes*, University of Kansas Humanistic Studies 53 (Lawrence: University of Kansas Publications, 1981).

INTRODUCTION

Literary theory and hermeneutics have had great difficulty giving any satisfactory treatment of "meaning." On the one hand, the volumes of argument about the meaning of texts, from the formalist theory of W. K. Wimsatt to the deconstructionist theory of Jacques Derrida, seem not to have inhibited the discussion of "what the author intended" or "the meaning of the text" in most literature courses. On the other hand, the recent preoccupation of literary studies with creating and defending theories of literature has made it necessary that any convincing treatment of meaning be a linguistical-philosophical-epistemological-phenomenological-ontological analysis that resolves the disputes and disagreements about meaning among the various formalist, structuralist, deconstructionist, hermeneutical theories of literary art. Therefore both the utility and the feasibility of an adequate treatment of meaning are questionable.

Moreover, an aura of naïveté surrounds one who is overly concerned with "meaning" in literature. After all, questions of meaning tend to disappear as theoretical disciplines become more sophisticated. Natural science stopped talking about "final causes," that is, the purpose and meaning of things and events in the world, in the seventeenth century. Purpose and meaning seemed irrelevant to their aim, which was prediction and control. Linguistics and behavioral studies, which have come of age in the twentieth century, have similarly defined themselves in ways that seem to clear an area in which they can study language and human behavior not primarily to interpret their meaning, but to discover the hidden, underlying systems and laws that govern them. The fate of meaning has been the same in literary theory and criticism that take linguistics and science as models of inquiry. After Jonathan Culler and Roland Barthes and Jacques Derrida, how can one raise the overwhelming question of the meaning of a text? After Jeffrey Stout's cogent appeal, in a recent issue of *New Literary History*, for the elimination of the term "meaning" from our talk about texts, why persist in writing a book about meaning?

In spite of these intimidations, I have intrepidly set out to review and perhaps to help shape the fate of meaning in contemporary theory about literature and interpretation. I have written from the perspective of one who assigns a central importance in human life to literary art on the grounds that it does express meaning, who wants to make that perspective tenable for others, and who thinks that if our mode of inquiry causes us to scorn the search for meaning in literature, then both our mode of inquiry and our search need to be reassessed.

Wallace Stevens, the American poet, wrote: "After the final no there comes a yes / And on that yes the future world depends."[1] These two lines of poetry serve well to summarize this study. First, I attempt to pose forcefully, succinctly, and accurately the insights that have undercut the authority and certainty of all acts of perception and interpretation, that is, all acts of assigning or discovering meaning in literature. The "final no" at which we have arrived in our quest for meaning is not a statement of rebellion like the "everlasting no" of Diogenes Teufelsdrochk in Carlyle's *Sartor Resartus*, or the refusal to recant of Galileo, or the "I will not serve" of Satan in

---

[1] "The Well Dressed Man with a Beard," *The Collected Poems of Wallace Stevens* (New York: Alfred A. Knopf, 1965), p. 247.

Milton's *Paradise Lost*. Rather, it is an admission of a loss of faith in the ability of our rational systems to lead us to any objectively determinable meanings. That admission seems to be the logical conclusion reached through a sophisticated understanding of the nature of language and by all the theoretical disciplines.

After presenting a critique of current trends in theory that are reshaping, unsettling, problematizing, and discrediting our conceptions of literature and criticism, I offer an alternative theory that gives to interpreters (which we all are since we never achieve a preinterpretive perspective) grounds for certainty and authority and freedom. The "yes" of this section is made possible by a shift in perspective that does not refute what drove us to the admission of the indeterminacy and uncertainty of our knowledge but allows us to see differently, to build new and better worlds.

Two fundamental assumptions inform this study. The first is that any convincing theory of meaning must be given in the context of a theory of language. The "linguistic turn" in twentieth-century thought that sees language as the medium of all human experience and knowledge makes a theory of language fundamental to an investigation of meaning, and of anything else for that matter. The expressions that have become catchphrases for expressing the centrality of language, such as *"The limits of my language* mean the limits of my world" and "Being that can be understood is language,"[2] reveal that, before we can study the world or being, we must have a conception of language with which to work. The goal of this study is presumptuous: to challenge that conception of language which appears to me to be functioning as an "un-

---

[2] Ludwig Wittgenstein, *Tractatus Logico-Philosophicus*, trans. D. F. Pears and B. F. McGuinness (London: Routledge & Kegan Paul, 1961), p. 115, and Hans-Georg Gadamer, "Foreword to the Second Edition," *Truth and Method* (New York: Seabury Press, 1975), p. xxiii, respectively.

broken myth" underlying literary theory and conditioning any treatment of meaning.

The second fundamental assumption informing this work is that any theory of language is based on a definition of a sign and its relations to other signs. Ferdinand de Saussure gave such a definition, although he predicted the emergence of a new science that would more adequately "show what constitutes signs, what laws govern them."[3] Modern linguistics and semiological studies have made gigantic strides in analyzing systems of relations using Saussure's definition; apparently, however, not much more is known today about "what constitutes signs, what laws govern them" than Saussure knew seventy-five years ago, if one judges by the fact that his definition is still the standard one. Charles S. Peirce, Saussure's American contemporary, also offered a definition of a sign and the laws governing signs. He called his theory of signs "semiotic." I contend that the treatment of meaning and related questions has been essentially the working out of what is already implied in these two basic definitions of a sign. As a heuristic device for the purposes of this study, I use Saussurean linguistics and Peircean semiotics as two fundamentally different starting points for the study of meaning. I face two challenges in using this approach. The first is to present some basic information about Saussure's linguistics, which is necessary to make clear my subsequent arguments, without boring the reader with what is already very familiar. I can only say that I provide the bare essentials in a short space. This section is clearly marked in Chapter 1 with the subtitle "Saussure's General Linguistics" and may be skipped by those familiar with Saussure's work. The other challenge is of a different nature. Peirce's theory of signs is so unfamiliar to most readers and so intimidating to many others that I am compelled to

[3] Ferdinand de Saussure, *Course in General Linguistics*, ed. Charles Bally and Albert Sechehaye, trans. Wade Baskin (New York: McGraw-Hill, 1959), p. 16.

provide an introduction to Peirce's theory of signs as a "new" linguistic model and show its potentially revolutionary implications for literary studies in order to carry out the critique of meaning that is central to this book.

Part One will review briefly (1) Saussure's fundamental concepts and terms that underlie his linguistic theory, and (2) the implications of his theory for meaning as they have been worked out by literary theorists. I do not make any argument about the originality, uniqueness, or even the influence of Saussure. It is well known that several of Saussure's contemporaries, notably Sigmund Freud and Emile Durkheim, living in different parts of the world and unknown to each other, arrived at some of the same structural principles Saussure defined in his linguistic theory. I begin with Saussure because his theory of language as a system of signs has offered the starting point, the terminology, and often the subject for much of what has been written about language and interpretation up to the present time.

By emphasizing the difficulties in treating meaning that are encountered by theorists inspired by Saussurean linguistics, I do not mean to berate the contributions of structuralist and poststructuralist theorists. The influence they have had is almost inestimable. In 1945 Ernst Cassirer said that the rise of the science of linguistics "may very well be compared to the new science of Galileo which in the seventeenth century changed our whole concept of the physical world."[4] In that same year, the anthropologist Claude Lévi-Strauss said that Saussurean linguistics "ought to play the same renovating role for the social sciences that nuclear physics, for example, played for the exact sciences."[5] Cassirer and Lévi-Strauss were seem-

[4] Ernst Cassirer, "Structuralism in Modern Linguistics," *Word* 1 (1945): 99; cited in Jonathan Culler, *The Pursuit of Signs* (London: Routledge & Kegan Paul, 1981), p. 24.

[5] Claude Lévi-Strauss, *Anthropologie structurale* (Paris: Plon, 1958), p. 40; cited in Culler, *The Pursuit of Signs*, p. 28.

ingly prophetic. Whether or not the "renovating role" of linguistics is the cause, we find the structural principles of linguistics not only in the anthropology of Lévi-Strauss, the sociology of Durkheim, the psychoanalysis of Freud, the socioeconomic theory of Karl Marx, but also in the philosophy of science of Thomas Kuhn. And the list could go on. Saussure's theory of language is either consistent with or has given rise to what has become the prevailing worldview of the Western world.

However, the analogies used by Cassirer and Lévi-Strauss, comparing linguistics with both classical and modern science, are insightful in a way other than that of showing the importance of Saussure's contribution. Saussurean linguistics incorporates the subject-object dualism of classical science and the indeterminacy of quantum mechanics. All three share a fundamental predisposition to see everything in dualistic, dyadic, binary terms, and that influences their perceptions even when they call into question such a predisposition.

Part Two begins with a review of Charles S. Peirce's theory of signs and proceeds to give an account of the nature of language and meaning in literary art, criticism, and theory according to his theory. Peirce's semiotic is the working out of a theory of language based on a definition of a sign as triadic. The Peircean perspective provides a clarification and critique of the treatment of meaning by theorists whose work has typically been categorized as formalist, structuralist, deconstructionist, or hermeneutic theory. Many theorists, such as Roland Barthes, Stanley Fish, Jacques Derrida, have recognized the shortcomings of structural linguistics as a model for literary theory and have offered critiques of it, but in most cases they do not escape from the basic conception of a sign as dyadic, the implications of which Saussure's theory is merely the working out. Deconstruction is very much in the Saussurean tradition of thinking about signs.

In a preface to his *Collected Papers* Charles Peirce says his undertaking is to "outline a theory so comprehensive that, for a long time to come, the entire work of human reason, in philosophy of every school and kind, in mathematics, in psychology, in physical science, in history, in sociology, and whatever other department there may be, shall appear as the filling up of its details."[6] Peirce was not only immodest but also wrong in his prediction about the impact of his theory. The question of why Peirce, who devoted a lifetime to the study of signs and who was, according to many historians of ideas, "the most original, versatile, and comprehensive philosophical mind this country has yet produced,"[7] has had so little impact on literary studies, at least until recently, deserves careful study. There are many possible reasons. Whether because of his extensive use of unfamiliar terms and what he called his "left-handed" way of thinking, because his own interest was primarily in logic rather than in literature or linguistics, because much of his writing on signs was left in letters and manuscripts that were not published until many years after his death in 1914 (some of his manuscripts are still unpublished), or because of any number of other stylistic, biographical, and historical facts, Peirce's theory has not inspired the reassessment he envisioned. But he may not have been wrong about the potential of his theory. At present, after the thoroughgoing critique of structuralist theory by Jacques Derrida and other deconstructionists, after the efforts by Martin Heidegger, Hans-Georg Gadamer, Ludwig Wittgenstein, and others to break out of the objectivist, dualistic mindsets of scientific methodology, the time may have finally arrived when the semiotic of Peirce can provide a frame of reference that will

[6] *The Collected Papers of Charles Sanders Peirce*, vols. 1–6, ed. Charles Hartshorne and Paul Weiss, 1931–1935; vols. 7–8, ed. A. W. Burks, 1958 (Cambridge: Harvard University Press, 1931), vol. 1, p. vii.

[7] Ernest Nagel, *Scientific American* 200 (1959): 185; cited in *Writings of Charles S. Peirce: A Chronological Edition*, ed. Edward C. Moore et al. (Bloomington: Indiana University Press, 1984), vol. 2, p. xi.

allow us to get outside, not of language, but of a theory of language that has come to be seen as inadequate and divorced from the practice of the very activities it supposedly explains.

The questions that have preoccupied literary theorists—questions about author's intention, the autonomy of the text, the role of the reader, the nature of language, the source and nature of meaning—have quite different answers depending on the definition of a sign with which we begin. My first thesis is that if you are in search of meaning and you begin with a Saussurean, dyadic definition of a sign, "You can't get there from here," to use the language of advice we usually ignore. My second thesis is that if you begin your search for meaning with a Peircean definition of a sign, "You can't miss it if you just keep going."

PART ONE

▽

The Fate of Meaning in Structuralist Literary Theory

The nightingale won no prize at the poultry show.

—Sir Walter Raleigh

ONE

Beginning with Saussure: The Sentence-Text Analogy

That inscrutable thing is chiefly what I hate.

—Ahab in Herman Melville, *Moby Dick*

Presumably the first step in considering the fate of meaning in literary theory would be to define meaning. However, it is the persistent inability of linguists, philosophers, and hermeneutical and literary theorists to give a satisfactory definition of meaning that is the impetus for this study. Charlton Laird, in his prefatory article in *Webster's New World Dictionary*, puts the case succinctly: "nobody knows what meaning is or how to define it."[1] Couple that with W. V. Quine's statement that, "pending a satisfactory explanation of the notion of meaning, linguists in the semantic fields are in the situation of not knowing what they are talking about,"[2] and we seem to be driven to the conclusion stated by Jeffrey Stout: "If interpretation is a matter of discovering meaning, and is therefore bound to run amuck when informed by mistaken assumptions about what meaning is, then literary criticism, religious

[1] "Language and Meaning," *Webster's New World Dictionary of the American Language*, 2nd ed. (New York: William Collins & World Publishing Co., 1974), p. xxvi.

[2] W. V. Quine, "The Problem of Meaning in Linguistics," *From a Logical Point of View: Logico-Philosophical Essays* (Cambridge: Harvard University Press, 1964), p. 47.

3

studies, classics, history—in short, all disciplines involving the interpretation of texts—will consist largely in failure to deliver promised goods."[3] Stout's proposed solution is that, at least in hermeneutical theory and literary criticism, we quit talking about the meaning of texts altogether.

In the wake of such thinking about meaning, which seems to be representative, the effort to contribute to a satisfactory notion of meaning must begin with a review of the assumptions and theories on which such thinking is based. Some contend, Martin Heidegger among others, that the inability of theoretical disciplines, including literary theory, to deal with meaning is inherent in the analytical mode of thinking that for heuristic purposes divides the world into subjects and objects, which are then thought of as independent entities. So long as language and texts are treated as institutions or artifacts existing as systems or objects independent of persons, events, and other objects, we will not be able to talk intelligently about their meanings. This seems to be what has happened in most of the literary theory that takes its start from Saussure and linguistics.

Without pretending to give a comprehensive treatment of structuralism or deconstruction, I intend to show in this and the subsequent two chapters that the treatment of meaning in structural and deconstructive theories is merely the working out of what is implicit in Saussure's definition of the linguistic sign. This portion of the study will culminate in an analysis of the work of Jacques Derrida because he has dealt so thoroughly and insightfully with meaning. Derrida's deconstruction is not so much a theory or system as it is a method of critiquing theory. Whereas structuralists have attempted to treat the structure of content, Derrida's project is to treat the

---

[3] Jeffrey Stout, "What Is the Meaning of a Text?" *New Literary History* 14 (Autumn 1982): 1.

structurality of structure. Derrida says that although structurality has always been at work, it has been overlooked because of the assumption that there is within the structure a center, a truth that governs, but is not itself, structurality.

Structuralists take meaning as a given, a center, a point of reference, then try to identify the system of codes responsible for the accepted meaning. Derrida's project is to deconstruct this center, this meaning, which he calls the transcendental signified—"transcendental" because it is conceived of as a concept independent of language, an ideality exterior to the process of language, a something that language means to say. Rather than seeing meaning as a center that governs structure, Derrida sees it as coming after, a product of, structurality.

I assume that I may well have lost some of my readers in the last two paragraphs because of all the abstract terms: deconstruction, structurality, and transcendental signified. For these readers the following, very brief review of basic linguistic and structural theory will make my discussion of the treatment of meaning in structural and poststructural thought much clearer.

SAUSSURE'S GENERAL LINGUISTICS

Between the years 1906 and 1911, at the University of Geneva, Ferdinand de Saussure offered three times a course in general linguistics. A book made from notes taken by students in the course was published in 1915, after the death of Saussure. This book, entitled *Course in General Linguistics*, laid the foundation for the study of language in the twentieth century and provided the concepts and terms for a theory of structuralism, the implications of which have amounted to a revolutionary change in our perceptions of the the world and of ourselves.

Saussure began by fencing off language, defining an object to be studied as independent from both the users of language and the world of existent reality. Language, he said, is a system of signs, the most important among many such systems. Language as a system Saussure called *la langue*. The actual manifestations of language in speech he called *la parole*. *Langue* is an institution, a set of impersonal rules and conventions, "a self-contained whole and a principle of classification."[4] One must have assimilated ("passively assimilated" in one's native language) the rules and conventions in order to speak a language. *Parole* is language as it is used in speaking. English utterances, for example, are the only data the linguist has about the underlying system, the English *langue*. Saussure's fundamental notion was that for any words or speech acts to have meaning there must be a system that makes it possible to utter and understand them.[5]

To illustrate the relationship of *langue* and *parole*, Saussure used as an analogy the distinction "between the abstract set of rules and conventions called 'chess' and the actual concrete games of chess played by people in the real world." Although Saussure refers to this analogy several times, he never states it as concisely as does Terence Hawkes, whom I quote here:

> The rules of chess can be said to exist above and beyond each individual game, but they only ever acquire concrete form in the relationships that develop between the pieces in individual games. So with language. The nature of the *langue* lies beyond and determines the nature of each manifestation of *parole*, yet it has no concrete existence of its own, except in the piecemeal manifestations that speech affords.[6]

[4] Saussure, *Course in General Linguistics*, ed. Charles Bally and Albert Sechehaye, trans. Wade Baskin (New York: McGraw-Hill, 1959), p. 9.

[5] Ibid., pp. 7–17.

[6] Hawkes, *Structuralism and Semiotics* (Berkeley: University of California Press, 1977), pp. 20–21. See also Saussure, *Course in General Linguistics*, pp. 22–23, 88–89, 110.

Parole could have no meaning if there were no *langue* to make *parole* and meaning possible; yet there is no *langue* except as manifested in *parole*. Thus, linguistics has its mission to study *parole* in order to understand the *langue* that makes *parole* possible.

The focus of the linguist, then, is not upon what a certain sign means, but upon the system, the structure of the system, that makes a conventional meaning possible. The shift of emphasis is from *what* something means to *how* it means. Having made the distinction between *langue* and *parole*, Saussure is interested in *parole* insofar as it leads him to an understanding of *langue*. His concern is with what is "social" rather than individual, with what "never requires premeditation" rather than with what is "wilful and intellectual," with what is "essential" rather than what is "more or less accidental," with the system that makes possible a particular speech act rather than with a particular speech act.[7]

The implications of the distinction between *langue* and *parole* are numerous. Most notable for our study of meaning is the fundamental assumption that if any sign has meaning there must be a system that allows it to have meaning. But what is a sign, and how does the system work?

Saussure said that the linguistic sign "is a two-sided psychological entity" composed of a "concept and a sound-image":

> I call the combination of a concept and a sound-image a *sign*, but in current usage the term generally designates only a sound-image. . . . I propose to retain the word *sign* [*signe*] to designate the whole and to replace *concept* and *sound-image* respectively by *signified* [*signifié*] and *signifier* [*signifiant*]; the last two terms have the advantage of indicating the opposition that separates them from each other and from the whole of which they are parts. . . .

[7] *Course in General Linguistics*, p. 14.

The linguistic sign, as defined, has two primordial characteristics. In enunciating them I am also positing the basic principles of any study of this type.[8]

The first of the basic principles to which Saussure refers is that the relationship between the signifier and the signified is arbitrary. The term "arbitrary," he points out, "should not imply that the choice of the signifier is left entirely to the speaker (... the individual does not have the power to change a sign in any way once it has become established in the linguistic community)."[9] Rather it means that the signifier-signified relationship is "unmotivated"; that is, there is no "natural connection" or any intrinsic reason why a particular sound-image should be linked with a particular concept. There is no reason why "tree" rather than "Baum" should be linked to the concept of that thing Joyce Kilmer thought more lovely than a poem.

It is integral to Saussure's theory that although signs are arbitrary they are immutable:

> The signifier, though to all appearances freely chosen with respect to the idea that it represents, is fixed, not free, with respect to the linguistic community that uses it. The masses have no voice in the matter, and the signifier chosen by language could be replaced by no other. ... No individual, even if he willed it, could modify in any way at all the choice that has been made; and what is more, the community itself cannot control so much as a single word; it is bound to the existing language.[10]

But even though signifiers are immutable for users of the language and are a heritage from the preceding period, language

---

[8] Ibid., pp. 66–67.
[9] Ibid., pp. 68–69.
[10] Ibid., p. 71.

changes. Shifts in the relation of signifiers and signifieds occur not through the control or will of users, but through use, the circulation and life of the language over a period of time.

The immutability of language for the users of language and the mutability of language over time calls, according to Saussure, for two branches of linguistics—synchronic and diachronic. Saussure felt that linguistics up to his time had been totally diachronic, or historical, linguistics. He did not reject the value of historical linguistics, but asserted that "the diachronic perspective deals with phenomena that are unrelated to systems although they do condition them."[11] And when one is trying to reconstruct the system of language that gives signs their value and function, he or she must "discard all knowledge of everything that produced it and ignore diachrony."[12] Language is a system of interrelated units, and the value of those units is determined by their places in the system at a given time and in a given state, rather than by their history. Saussure again uses the chess analogy to illustrate the point:

> . . . one who has followed the entire match has no advantage over the curious party who comes up at a critical moment to inspect the state of the game; to describe this arrangement, it is perfectly useless to recall what has just happened ten seconds previously. . . . The changes that intervene between states have no place in either state.[13]

Thus, Saussure laid the theoretical foundation for synchronic, or "structural," analyses, which attempt to describe systems without respect to time. It was this shift in perspective that Lévi-Strauss saw as the "renovating" lesson that linguistics offered to anthropology and other disciplines.

Finally, Saussure must describe the synchronic "relations and differences" among linguistic signs in the system. He said

[11] Ibid., p. 85.
[12] Ibid., p. 81.
[13] Ibid., p. 89.

that "combinations supported by linearity are *syntagms*. . . . In a syntagm a term acquires its value only because it stands in opposition to everything that precedes or follows it, or to both."[14] Thus, relations of signs in sequence are called syntagmatic. Signs in a linguistic series also carry with them values from oppositions and relations that are "outside discourse"; these values are "not supported by linearity" but are the contrasts of a sign with other signs that might replace it in a linguistic series. Such relations, which Saussure called "associative" relations, are now commonly described as "paradigmatic."

A moment's reflection on Saussure's distinctions between *langue* and *parole*, signifier and signified, synchronic and diachronic, syntagmatic and paradigmatic, reveals that they are formal and heuristic. In the use of language we are unconscious of the distinctions; and in our efforts to study language as phenomena, both parts of the antinomies are always given together. However, the validity of the distinctions has been unchallenged for the most part, and Saussure's theory has provided the theoretical basis for most "structuralist" and "poststructuralist" literary theory.[15] The prevailing orthodoxy that has emerged is that in language there are only differences

[14] Ibid., p. 123.

[15] For the purpose of this study, which is not to classify or compare the differing methods and goals of various theorists and schools of theory, but to show that the fate of meaning in all language theory is prefigured by the definition of a sign with which theorists begin, I use the term "structuralism" in the broad sense defined by Jonathan Culler in *On Deconstruction: Theory and Criticism after Structuralism* to designate all theorists who "take linguistics as a model and attempt to develop 'grammars'—systematic inventories of elements and their possible combination—that would account for the form and meaning of literary works" ([Ithaca, N.Y.: Cornell University Press, 1982], p. 22). Poststructuralism, although it investigates and undermines the conclusions of earlier structuralists, can be seen as part of structuralism in this broad sense because it, too, claims to be a working out of what is implicit in Saussurean linguistics. In Part Two, I sometimes use "structuralism" to refer to all theory based on Saussurean linguistics, but that usage will be clear in context.

without positive terms.[16] A sign has no meaning in itself but has meaning in relation to other signs. Consequently, meaning depends on the system, on the oppositions and contrasts within the system. To understand what and how something means, we must reconstruct the system of which it is a part.

One can find a similar set of assumptions in the structuralist theory of the social sciences, whether one looks at the anthropology of Lévi-Strauss, the psychoanalytic theory of Freud, or the sociology of Durkheim. They all assume structures, foundations, and attitudes outside of conscious awareness that are the structures the mind imposes on perception. When we seem to be dealing with facts of nature, they say, we are subconsciously using a structuring system of signs. Whether these systems be social ideologies, languages, or structures of the preconscious, they are the media in which we live and move and have our being.

THE SENTENCE-TEXT ANALOGY

What kind of literary study does structuralist thinking lead to? The answer is that structuralist poetics is simply the application to literature of the ideas about language defined above. Since literature is language, the argument goes, the structures and elements of literature must be homogeneous with those of language. Thus literature is viewed as a self-generating, self-regulating, self-referring system. Its parts, whether individual works of literary art or words within a particular text, depend not on anything outside of literature for meaning but depend on intertextual and intratextual relations. Literary language calls attention to itself as symbol and declares itself *not* to offer an unmediated experience of world, people, places, and events that the use of ordinary language seems to offer. Thus, literature like language is seen as

[16] *Course in General Linguistics*, p. 120.

a system of signs independent of anything outside itself; but, unlike ordinary language, it calls attention to its own fictional, arbitrary, symbolic nature. The primary difference between literature and the everyday use of language is that literature somehow "knew all along" what has been said in the previous section about language being a system of signs. Because a literary work is self-consciously "fictional," literature has the status of being the only form of language free from the illusion that it refers to "reality." Literature has always known, the structuralist says, that which has revolutionized the social sciences in the twentieth century. Literature declares that the signs of which it is constituted do not depend for their meaning on correspondence to any empirical reality.[17]

There is, of course, no uniform agreement about what the linguistic model shows us about the nature of literature. However, there is near consensus about the fate of meaning in structural literary theory. The next several pages will spell out that fate in some detail.

Jonathan Culler, in the preface to his book *Structuralist Poetics*, gives a description of the kind of literary study structuralist thinking leads to:

> The type of literary study which structuralism helps one to envisage would not be primarily interpretive; it would not offer a method which, when applied to literary works, produced new and hitherto unexpected meanings. Rather than a criticism which discovers and assigns meanings, it would be a poetics which strives to define the conditions of meaning. Granting new attention to the activity of reading, it would attempt to specify how we go about making sense of texts, what are the interpretive operations on which literature itself, as an institution, is based.... The study of literature, as opposed to the pe-

[17] Hawkes, *Structuralism and Semiotics*, p. 86.

rusal and discussion of individual works, would attempt to understand the conventions which make literature possible.[18]

Three characteristics of a structuralist literary study stand out clearly in Culler's statement. First, he says it is not one that "discovers or assigns meanings." Second, such a literary study does not focus on individual works, but on the "conditions of meaning," the *langue* of literature. Third, a literary study based on the possible relations between literary and linguistic studies will grant "new attention to the activity of reading." This third point is understated: the act of reading has perhaps become the primary focus of literary theory.

As might be expected from what Culler did say, he did not mention the author. A method of literary study that declares itself not concerned with meaning or with individual works but with the act of reading can ignore the author and the author's intention. The New Criticism, with its focus on the finished work itself, had already dealt extensively with the relation of the artist to the work. For example, W. K. Wimsatt, Jr., and Monroe Beardsley in their essay "The Intentional Fallacy" argue that the intention of the author is neither available nor desirable as a standard for interpreting literature.[19] And when structuralists announced "The Death of the Author,"[20] they stated only what was implicit in Saussurean linguistics. To the structuralist, in this case Roland Barthes, the author is "never more than the instance writing, just as *I* is

[18] *Structuralist Poetics: Structuralism, Linguistics, and the Study of Literature* (Ithaca, N.Y.: Cornell University Press, 1975), p. viii.

[19] In W. K. Wimsatt, Jr., *The Verbal Icon: Studies in the Meaning of Poetry* (Lexington: University of Kentucky Press, 1948), pp. 3–18.

[20] This is a title of a chapter in Roland Barthes, *Image, Music, Text*, trans. Stephen Heath (New York: Hill & Wang, 1978), pp. 142–148. Michel Foucault and Claude Lévi-Strauss have also treated extensively the function and status of the human in determining meaning.

nothing other than the instance saying *I*: language knows a 'subject,' not a 'person.'" When one reads, there is language, not an author "with a being preceding and exceeding the writing." The author "is not subject with the book as predicate.... Every text is eternally written here and now."[21] The text is a space where a variety of writings, none of them original with the author, blend and clash. It employs, combines, contrasts numerous cultural codes, and they are all far richer than the author's awareness of them. Even if we had any way of knowing the author's awareness of the various codes, which we do not, that would not necessarily limit the possible meanings of the work. Umberto Eco's statement in his book *The Role of the Reader* is typical: "I ... renounce the use of the term /author/ if not as a mere metaphor for 'textual strategy.'"[22]

If we begin with the assumption that meaning is explained in terms of systems of signs—systems that persons do not control—then the systems of signs rather than the individual are the source of meaning. The status of an author's role as the giver of meaning is called into question by the same logic that says most people know and use a language but would need a linguist to tell them what it is they know that enables them to use the language. We know how to live in a culture, we use and read body language, but we need a social scientist to tell us what we know that makes this possible. The author, likewise, has a limited awareness of the systems that make his or her work possible.

Because of the linguistic model that defines language as an independent system, and a sign as arbitrary in essence but as fixed convention within the system, the structuralist begins by scrutinizing conventional meanings "already known or attested within the culture in hopes of discovering the conven-

---

[21] Barthes, "The Death of the Author," *Image, Music, Text*, p. 145.
[22] *The Role of the Reader: Explorations in the Semiotics of Texts* (Bloomington: Indiana University Press, 1979), p. 11.

tions which members of that culture have mastered."[23] Culler says that

> just as the speaker of a language has assimilated a complex grammar which enables him to read a series of sounds or letters as a sentence with meaning, so the reader of literature has acquired, through his encounters with literary works, implicit mastery of various semiotic conventions which enable him to read a series of sentences as poems or novels endowed with shape and meaning.[24]

Consequently, in the study of literature the structuralist tries to "describe the system of conventions which enable poems to have the meaning (the range of meanings) they do."[25] Just as the linguist does not propose new meanings for sentences, the structuralist does not seek to determine the true meaning of poems. His task is descriptive, not prescriptive and evaluative. He concerns himself not with how texts are constructed or with what authors intend or with any other genetic concerns that are outside the language of the text, but with what is given, including the meaning of the text.[26]

But if theorists by using the linguistic model could explain *how* texts have the meanings they do, that would be a significant contribution to any theory of meaning. Several efforts to provide such an explanation are based on the assumption that narratives must have a grammar just as sentences do. Tzvetan

[23] Jonathan Culler, "The Semiotics of Poetry: Two Approaches," *Semiotic Themes*, ed. Richard T. DeGeorge (Lawrence: University of Kansas Publications, 1981), p. 92.

[24] Culler, *Structuralist Poetics*, p. viii.

[25] Culler, "The Semiotics of Poetry," p. 89.

[26] Ibid. Culler, *On Deconstruction*, p. 223: "to get its analytic projects underway, structuralism must provide a new center, a given that can serve as point of reference. This given is *meaning*.... Taking meanings as given, poetics tries to identify the system of codes responsible for these accepted and acceptable meanings."

Todorov, for example, claims that "the notion itself of a grammar of narrative cannot be contested. This notion rests on the profound unity of language and narrative."[27] In his essay "The Grammar of Narrative" Todorov sets forth what he finds to be the narrative grammar of Boccaccio's tales. For the primary parts of speech—common nouns, verbs, adjectives, adverbs, proper nouns, pronouns, articles—he finds parts of narrative. And just as these parts of speech have secondary properties (such as voice, tense, and mood) and form propositions, these parts of narrative have secondary properties and form narrative propositions. The syntactic units superior to propositions are sequences characterized by the type of relations between propositions. Here Todorov runs into trouble. He says, "If we seek to go beyond the level of propositions, more complex problems appear. For hitherto we could compare the results of our analysis with those of linguistic studies. But there is hardly any linguistic theory of discourse."[28]

The fact that linguistics does not provide a model for analyzing units larger than sentences forces Todorov into some awkward positions and ultimately calls into question the adequacy of the linguistic model for literary theory. For example, Todorov says that the first step in analyzing the grammar of narrative is to "present the plot in the form of a summary, in which each distinct action of the story has a corresponding proposition."[29] Surely it is fair to ask what is being analyzed, the grammar of the plot or that of the plot summary. Anticipating such criticism, Todorov says that his effort is not to explicate any particular narrative, or draw any conclusions from it, but that "our first task is the elaboration of a descrip-

---

[27] Todorov, "The Grammar of Narrative," *The Poetics of Prose*, trans. Richard Howard (Ithaca, N.Y.: Cornell University Press, 1977), p. 119.

[28] Ibid., p. 116.

[29] Ibid., pp. 118–119.

tive apparatus."[30] However, both of his fundamental assumptions, that there must be a grammar of narrative and that he can separate descriptive and interpretive acts, are based on the analogy of a sentence and a tale, an analogy that seems more and more faulty the further one pushes it.

Todorov's definition of the "fantastic" as a literary genre[31] encounters similar difficulties. Just as he defined narrative in terms of parts of speech, propositions, and sequences, he defines the fantastic genre in terms of verbal, syntactic, and semantic characteristics. In both cases his linguistic model fails him when he gets beyond the syntactic level.

Because of the limitations of the sentence-text analogy provided by the linguistic model, all efforts to discover the *langue* of literature are frustrated. Literary works have to be summarized, condensed, distorted, dissected, reduced to the forms that the model demands. Lévi-Strauss's study of myth, Vladimir Propp's study of folktales, A. J. Greimas's study of plot "paradigms" are all inadvertently reductionist efforts. The myths and tales with which they purportedly work are no more the referents of their systems than empirical reality is the referent of literature for a structuralist. And as Roland Barthes has pointed out, such studies seek to eliminate all differences among stories and constitute an entirely different project than the discovery of what meaning stories can have for readers and hearers.

Parenthetically, it is the sentence-text analogy that leads Stein H. Olsen and Jeffrey Stout, among others, to the conclusion that it is possible to talk about the meaning of a word, sentence, or utterance, but "pointless" and "fruitless" to talk about the meaning of a text.[32] Since the largest unit of lan-

[30] Ibid., p. 119.
[31] Todorov, *The Fantastic: A Structural Approach to a Literary Genre*, trans. Richard Howard (Ithaca, N.Y.: Cornell University Press, 1973).
[32] Olsen, "The 'Meaning' of a Literary Work," *New Literary History* 14 (Autumn 1982): 13–31; Stout, "What Is the Meaning of a Text?" pp. 1–12.

guage that linguistics describes is the sentence, we cannot talk about the structure and meaning of literary texts with any "theoretical perspicuity." One option is to stop talking about the meaning of texts, as Stout proposes. Another option is to hope, as Olsen does, that "literary theory will ... be able to break free from the semantic framework and the analogy between the literary work and basic linguistic expressions like metaphor, sentence, and utterance."[33] As I will show in Part Two, a literary theory based on Peirce's semiotic can treat the meaning of units larger than sentences.

Even though structural analyses based on the sentence-text analogy do not focus on meaning, the starting point of such analyses is the assumption that texts do have meaning—and since texts do have meaning, there must be a system. The concept of a text having meaning, as I will demonstrate in the next chapter, was challenged much more after theorists recognized the complex interrelationship of text and reader.

[33] Olsen, "The 'Meaning' of a Literary Work," p. 31.

TWO

The Reader/Text as Indeterminate

> There is only the fight to recover what has been
>   lost
> And found and lost again and again: and now,
>   under conditions
> That seem unpropitious. But perhaps neither gain
>   nor loss.
>
> —T. S. Eliot, "East Coker"

Roland Barthes in his later writings, while still acknowledging that his, and all, structural analyses of narrative have a single scientific origin—"semiology or the systematic study of signification"—moves away from the kind of structural analysis described in the previous chapter. He says that the effort "to see all the world's stories ... within a single structure" is "as exhausting ... as it is ultimately undesirable, for the text thereby loses its difference."[1] Moreover, he adds, such structural analysis "is particularly applicable to oral narrative," but "textual analysis" (the term Barthes applies to his own analysis) "is applicable exclusively to written narrative."[2] The following is Barthes' description of the kind of analysis he does in *S/Z* and in the article on Poe from which the statement is taken:

[1] Barthes, *S/Z*, trans. Richard Miller (New York: Hill & Wang, 1974), p. 3.
[2] Barthes, "Textual Analysis of a Tale by Edgar Poe," trans. Donald G. Marshall, *Poe Studies* 10 (June 1977): 2.

Textual analysis does not try to *describe* the structure of a work ... but rather to produce a moving structuration of the text (a structuration which displaces itself from reader to reader throughout the length of history).... We ... therefore take a narrative text, and ... read it, as slowly as necessary, stopping as often as necessary ... attempting to mark and to class *without rigor* not all the senses of the text (that would be impossible, for the text is open to infinity: no reader, no subject, no systematic study can stop the text) but the forms, the codes, according to which senses are possible. We ... mark the *approaches* of sense. Our aim is not to find *the* sense, nor even *a* sense of the text, and our labor is no kin to literary criticism of a hermeneutic type (which seeks to interpret the text according to the truth it thinks is kept concealed in it).... Our goal is to come to conceive, imagine, live the plural of the text, the opening of its signifying.[3]

Even though Barthes calls what he does *textual* analysis, the status of the text in such analysis is about as nebulous as that of "sense." He does not seek to find anything, structure or sense, *in* the text. He seeks a "moving structuration," "*approaches* of sense." Implicit in Barthes' rejection of earlier structural analysis is the judgment that they were simplistic in their conceptions of the *langue* of narrative and in their presumed objectivity; the structures are not stable and fixed *in* the text, but are dynamic and in process of becoming *in the reading* of the text.

Barthes and reader-response theorists shift their focus from the text to the relation-of-the-reader-to-the-text. Numerous efforts have been made to clarify the nature of the relationship of the reader to the text. Umberto Eco distinguishes between "open" and "closed" texts. A closed text, such as Superman comics, can be read by almost any reader and interpreted in a

---

3 Ibid.

multitude of different ways. From such a text, Eco asserts, one may infer what kind of audience the author had in mind, but not what requirements a good reader of the text should meet. An "open" text, on the other hand, requires a "Model Reader as a component of its structural strategy."[4] The model reader is determined by the interpretive operations he or she must be able to perform in order to cooperate with the textual strategies of the work. According to Eco, "when reading *Ulysses* one can extrapolate the profile of a 'good *Ulysses* reader' from the text itself."[5] Roland Barthes distinguishes between "writerly" and "readerly" texts. Writerly texts, he says, are ones that "make the reader no longer a consumer, but a producer of the text." The writerly text "can be written (rewritten) today," "is a perpetual present," "is *ourselves writing*." Readerly texts are ones that "can be read, but not written"; they are "products" that leave the reader "with no more than the poor freedom either to accept or reject the text."[6] Michael Riffaterre, in his *Semiotics of Poetry*, and Wolfgang Iser, in *The Implied Reader* and *The Act of Reading*, also try to show how texts set up certain requirements for the reader or guide the reader by the blanks and negations left for him or her to fill in.

Such analyses become very complex and difficult for reasons that are plain enough. They assume that two entities come together (reader and text), each defined as so many symbol systems, codes, and strategies, and they wish to define the contribution of each to a new entity—the text as read. One of my students used the following image to conceive of the situation. It is as if the reader brings to the text a large stained-glass window that has a pattern and many varicolored panes (representing the strategies, codes, and forms that make up his way of seeing). The text he wishes to read is another such

---

[4] Eco, *The Role of the Reader: Explorations in the Semiotics of Texts* (Bloomington: Indiana University Press, 1979), p. 9.

[5] Ibid.

[6] Barthes, *S/Z*, pp. 4–5.

window. He puts the windows face to face, holds them up to the light of interpretation, and sees the pattern and colors formed by the combination of the two. How can he determine what the contribution of each is to the pattern and colors that emerge? As Paul de Man points out, the situation is further complicated by the fact that the reader is no more constant than the text. Each time the reader interprets the text he changes it, and every change in the text makes a subsequent change in the reader.[7] The process is endless. Structuralists who focus on the reader-text relationship, then, find that the text and the meaning of the text are dynamic, constantly changing, in the process of becoming, not something fixed or static. A text is dynamic in that, like *langue* and *parole*, there is no text except in its various readings. And what any particular reader experiences in reading a text will be influenced by many things. How many social, political, artistic, and economic codes or systems does the reader bring to the text? How many other literary works has the reader read? What is the reader looking for? What is the circumstantial context in which the reader takes up the text? There are multiple possibilities of meaning, yet these possibilities are not infinite or controlled by any individual, author or reader.

Therefore, instead of focusing on the underlying grammar of the narrative, some structuralists (reader-response theorists) focus on the codes of literature and culture that make up the possible foreknowledge governing the insight and understanding of the reader. This assumed relationship of one's foreknowledge to his interpretation partially explains why the observation and interpretation of a text or anything else is always equally an observation of one's self. One's foreknowledge is always ahead of and controlling one's interpretation just as the scientist's apparatus is ahead of and controlling his

[7] De Man, *Blindness and Insight: Essays in the Rhetoric of Contemporary Criticism* (New York: Oxford University Press, 1971), p. 10.

observation of microparticles. Every observer must try but ultimately fail to separate himself from what he sees, or better
yet recognize himself in what he sees, or identify the methods,
values, and foreknowledge influencing his interpretation.
This being the case, Paul de Man has wryly suggested that the
psychoanalyst should pay half the fee because he is analyzing
himself as much as he is analyzing the patient.[8]

Even though reader-response theorists are primarily concerned with synchronic relations, the focus on the role of the
reader reintroduces the temporal dimension. Understanding
must be seen as a temporal act that has its own history and
context. Not only do interpretations of Shakespeare's plays
change from century to century, but they change from one
reading to the next. Thus, the notion of a "secret" or ultimate
meaning, from a reader's perspective, does not seem justifia-
ble.

Stanley Fish seems to offer the next logical step for the person who still wants to talk about "the meaning of texts." He
says that since it is futile to pretend that meaning or form or
author's intention is *in* the text, and since all we have to interpret are readings of the text, the proper place to look for
meaning is in the reader's experience of the text. Fish proposes
that the proper subject of interpretation is not the text, but
readers' activities, and suggests that we focus on them "not as
leading to meaning, but as *having* meaning."[9] Readers' activities, according to Fish, include the following:

> the making and revising of assumptions, the rendering
> and regretting of judgments, the coming to and aban-
> doning of conclusions, the giving and withdrawing of
> approval, the specifying of causes, the asking of ques-

[8] Ibid.

[9] Fish, "Interpreting the *Variorum*," *Is There a Text in This Class? The
Authority of Interpretive Communities* (Cambridge: Harvard University
Press, 1980), p. 158.

tions, the supplying of answers, the solving of puzzles. In a word, these activities are interpretive—rather than being preliminary to questions of value, they are at every moment settling and resettling questions of value—and because they are interpretive, a description of them will also be a description of a moving field of concerns, at once wholly present (not waiting for meaning but constituting meaning) and continually in the act of reconstituting itself.[10]

Fish's effort is to shift from a description of a text in "positivist, holistic, spatial" terms to a description of the experiencing of meaning in a temporal dimension. He rejects the perspective that treats the entire work as a single unit retrospectively, and embraces the perspective that describes what readers *do* as they read. The meanings of the work, Fish says, are the experiences the reader has in reading it. After taking a step toward conceiving of meaning as human experiences rather than as an object or a property of artifacts, he gets caught up in the questions that arise when the text is treated as an artifact. He ends up saying that interpretive communities make the texts have the meanings they do. "Interpretive communities," he says,

are made up of those who share interpretive strategies.... [T]hese strategies exist prior to the act of reading and therefore determine the shape of what is read rather than, as is usually assumed, the other way around.... The assumption in each community will be that the other is not correctly perceiving the "true text," but the truth will be that each perceives the text (or texts) its interpretive strategies demand and call into being. This, then, is the explanation both for the stability of interpretation among different readers (they belong to the same

[10] Ibid., pp. 158–159.

community) and for the regularity with which a single
reader will employ different interpretive strategies and
thus make different texts (he belongs to different communities).[11]

Fish cites Augustine's "rule of faith," given in *On Christian
Doctrine* as an example of a successful interpretive strategy.
Augustine argues (according to Fish) that "everything in the
Scripture, and indeed in the world when it is properly read,
points to (bears the meaning of) God's love for us and our
answering responsibility to love our fellow creatures for His
sake. If you come upon something which does not at first seem
to bear this meaning ... you are to take it 'to be figurative'
and to proceed to scrutinize it 'until an interpretation contrib-
uting to the reign of charity is produced.' "[12]

Even though Fish is trying to find a way to treat meaning,
the conception of interpretive strategies puts the experiencing-
of-the-text and its meaning out of reach just as his structuralist assumptions put the text and its meaning out of reach to
begin with. He supplants the text and its meaning with a textual strategy just as Todorov supplants Boccaccio's stories
with propositions. The actual text is no more the source of
meaning for Fish than the actual stories are the basis of Todorov's grammar of narrative. The interpretive strategy, as
defined by Fish, stipulates the meaning in advance and provides "a set of directions for finding it, which is of course a set
of directions ... for making it, that is, for the endless repro-
duction of the same text."[13]

In summary, having accepted as fact the impossibility of
objective, unmediated interpretation of texts, structuralists
and semiologists turned their attention to discovering the mediating systems for the text and reader, but of course their

[11] Ibid., p. 171.
[12] Ibid., p. 170.
[13] Ibid.

own theory precludes any objective study of them just as it precluded any objective study of individual texts. Despite the fact that Barthes' "textual analysis" and Fish's interpretive strategies and communities do not make accessible to us "the meaning of the text," they do illustrate something about the character of structural theory and help us to see why structuralism has not significantly enhanced our understanding of meaning.

Because of our structuralist assumptions, whatever we wish to study eludes us.[14] Everything that may have seemed objective, given, or having significance in itself is really already a part of a system that we brought to the perception of the thing perceived. What we come up with is exactly what our assumptions allow us to come up with—a sign within a system—and the significance of the sign changes as the system changes. The literary student who wants to study a text has no grounds on which the independence or objectivity of the thing studied can be established, since what he studies becomes a sign in the systems of signs that the student brings to the study.

Fish's description of interpretive strategies takes into account that the concepts of structuralism, like Augustine's interpretive program, tell us in advance what we will find regardless of what we look at. Not only are obstacles to the discovery of meaning built into structuralist thought, but so are obstacles to the discovery of anything except sign systems. Structural theory provides a very successful interpretive strategy. As Culler pointed out, structuralists take meaning as a given, a center, a point of reference, then try to identify the system of codes responsible for the accepted meaning. Therefore, if successful, they come out where they begin. It does not

[14] This is, of course, one of the fundamental points of the poststructural critique of structuralism. Jacques Derrida, whose work we will look at in some detail in Chapter 3, lists presence, science, history, and meaning among the things that elude us.

generate new meanings, but it cannot operate without accepted or conventional meanings.

While the understanding of language and of the limits it puts upon us has undergone radical revision, the concepts of meaning found in many structural analyses have not. Therefore, efforts to treat meaning, and the judgments made about the ability or inability of structuralist theory to treat meaning, often involve an archaic, objectivist notion of meaning as static entity and a conception of signs as dynamic, autonomous systems. In other words, meaning is still something other than signs, outside of or behind statements, in people rather than language; the working conception of meaning seems to be a holdover from an outmoded paradigm of language and reality. This is, of course, glimpsed by Barthes and Fish, who carefully stipulate that the archaic notion of meaning as fixed entity has no place in their analyses, but they do not provide an adequate substitute for it.

The complex problems with which Fish, Barthes, Eco, Riffaterre, Iser, and other reader-response theorists struggle are analogous to those that accompany modern physicists' attempts to determine simultaneously a particle's position and momentum. How can one bring together a notion of fixed meaning and an understanding of the dynamic nature of signs? The effort to see meaning as both fixed and dynamic is the major effort of contemporary literary theory.

Within the paradigm of structuralist theory the text and meaning are indeterminate in nature—both static and dynamic, signifier and signified, object and experience, actual expression and what is expressed, independent and dependent systems. And structural literary theory makes it impossible to separate the text, except arbitrarily, from such and such a reading of the text.

Since it is the purpose of Part One of this book to show why theories based on the Saussurean conception of a sign cannot give an adequate treatment of meaning, it may be

helpful to summarize our progress up to this point before analyzing the treatment of meaning in deconstruction and in
poststructural theory. I have tried to show that Ferdinand de
Saussure's insistence on the arbitrary nature of language made
meaning dependent on sign systems, on the relations and differences of signs. There is no meaning except through language and other sign systems. Structuralism makes the system
or structure of signs primordial—hence the efforts to find the
underlying systems, grammars, and competencies that are the
"real" sources of literary meaning or of any other knowledge.
Structuralists purport to be "scientific" and "objective" in the
study of literature and to tell us something about the structures of language, literature, and culture in general. I have
tried to demonstrate that their conclusions are vulnerable to
the same criticisms they had made of the New Critics; that is,
their objectivity is naïve and blind to the mediating influences
of all understanding.

Other structural analyses, particularly the reader-response
theorists discussed earlier in this chapter, acknowledge that
not only are cultural systems and codes earlier than texts, but
they are also earlier than authors and readers. Since the text
and the reading of the text are coeval insofar as they have
meaning, we must account for meaning by describing at least
the systems of the text *and* the reader. Paul de Man, in *Blindness and Insight*, while agreeing that the interpreter must try
to account for the intrusion and infusion of his own social self
into whatever he observes, shows the impossibility of ever separating the observer from the observed. Every interpretation
of one changes the other, and the process is seemingly endless.[15] Efforts of reader-response theorists to describe and explain objectively the interplay between the reader and text
merely displace the problem of meaning by changing the object of their inquiry; they do not deal satisfactorily with the

[15] De Man, *Blindness and Insight*, pp. 9–15.

inevitable blindness of their own subjectivity and method of questioning.

Stanley Fish's work exemplifies the effort to escape the implications of a theory of language without rejecting the theory itself. He tries to find a way to establish determinate meaning of particular works in spite of the obstacles posed by his own understanding of language. Fish admits that all we really have is our own subjective reading of the text, but, he says, subjectivity is really not very subjective: it is controlled by "interpretive strategies." Thus, interpretations are determined not by the author's intention or the text's structures, but by interpretive strategies, and their validity is attested to by the interpretive community that shares the interpretive strategy. In other words, for Fish to fix the reader's experience as the source of meaning, he must show the reader's experience to be something general rather than particular.[16]

The most insightful and sophisticated efforts to deal with the indeterminacy of binary oppositions in literary theory have been the work of the deconstructive theorists. The notions of trace, differ*a*nce, and supplement (to be defined more fully in the next chapter) all deal with the complexity, the necessity, the falsity, the indeterminacy of the binary system of signs in the structuralist paradigm.

Part of the poststructural or deconstructive critique of structuralism is that while it holds in theory that knowable reality is not in the mind or in the world, but is relational, is language, there still lurks a notion of a center, a reality outside of language, a user of language that exists independent of language, a reader of poetry who exists outside of poetry. Jacques

---

[16] E. D. Hirsch, Jr., whose work will be treated more fully in a later chapter, uses a similar strategy in his effort to establish determinate meaning. Hirsch claims that authorial intention, which had seemed to be discredited by structural theory, is the basis for establishing valid interpretations. He salvages authorial intention, so to speak, by finding it to be something general—type or genre—rather than something particular.

Derrida's critique of language and meaning argues that theorists such as Fish and Hirsch—despite their assumption that language is earlier than author, text, reader, or theorist—still hold to a traditional notion that the presence, origin, and clear sense of meaning can be attributed to the user of language. Therefore, they can equate meaning and intention, meaning and experience, meaning and conscious thought. They try to look into reality from a fixed place, to read as a fixed self, to take journeys but to keep track of a permanent address.

Douglas Hofstadter, in his book *Gödel, Escher, Bach*, gives us a story about Achilles and Tortoise, who have some "pushing-potion" that when drunk pushes them into a print of M. C. Escher; and if there is a print within that print, they can drink again and be pushed into it, and so on. They also have "popping-tonic" that allows them to pop out of the print they have popped into and that should allow them to pop back into reality. One problem Achilles and Tortoise have is that the world of every print feels as real as the reality from which they started. After pushing into a few of Escher's prints successively, they begin popping out, only to find that they have no way of knowing when they are back in the real world.[17] Jacques Derrida and other deconstructive or poststructural theorists have in essence said that we are all in the same position as Achilles and Tortoise, and that not only is it impossible to find our way back to the "real" world, there never was one. Consequently, structuralism can give no adequate treatment of meaning that is consistent with structuralist theory until it gives up the notion of fixed entities, whether these be realities independent of language, static identities, or fixed centers out of which we adventure into life. Meaning, somehow, must be conceived as relational, as language.

I have purposely not given a preview of the treatment of

[17] "Little Harmonic Labyrinth," *Gödel, Escher, Bach: An Eternal Golden Braid* (New York: Vintage Books, 1979), pp. 103–126.

meaning in Part Two of this work because it is not the new conception of meaning developed there that makes the treatment of meaning in structural theory inadequate. Rather, the treatment of meaning developed there (which stresses that meaning is not something in addition to language, that signs and meaning come together in our experience, that language/human action/world are inseparable, that meaning is a triadic relation that is inexpressible by means of dyadic relations alone) is offered in response to the thoroughgoing demonstration by persons working within the structuralist paradigm that theories based on the dyadic sign, the binary opposition, irreducible difference, cannot give an adequate treatment of meaning.

The achievement of poststructural theorists has been to knock the foundation out from under the structuralists while standing on their shoulders. That is, they show that there is no given, no center, no point of origin, but they continue to work within the structuralist paradigm based on a conception of the dyadic sign. They show us that not only is meaning indeterminate because of the nature of language, but the nature of language itself is indeterminate. Deconstruction is the "final no" to determinate meaning within the structuralist paradigm. But this statement is not a pejorative judgment of deconstruction or of the brilliant scholarship of those persons whose diverse contributions are lumped together under the umbrella term "deconstruction." Rather, it is a description of the fate of meaning in poststructuralist thought, as the next chapter will explain.

THREE

Meaning Endlessly Deferred

Why, today we don't even know where real life
is, what it is, or what it's called.

—Dostoyevsky, *Notes from Underground*

The purpose of this chapter is not to give an introduction to
or a review of deconstruction or poststructural literary theory,
since others have already done that better than I could,[1] but
to highlight the treatment of meaning in poststructural
thought. I want to show that certain assumptions about language prefigure the treatment of meaning in deconstruction
and to explain why deconstruction leaves us in despair of ever
having a theory of meaning, why I have called deconstruction
the "final no" to meaning—after which can come a yes. I will
refer extensively to the work of Jacques Derrida because Derrida has dealt so thoroughly and insightfully with these issues.
Of primary interest here is Derrida's treatment of determinate

[1] Some sympathetic and unsympathetic treatments of deconstruction that
I have found helpful are in the following works: G. Douglas Atkins, *Reading Deconstruction, Deconstructive Reading* (Lexington: University of Kentucky Press, 1983); Jonathan Culler, *On Deconstruction: Theory and Criticism
after Structuralism* (Ithaca, N.Y.: Cornell University Press, 1982); Terry
Eagleton, *Literary Theory: An Introduction* (Minneapolis: University of Min-
nesota Press, 1983); Christopher Norris, *Deconstruction: Theory and Practice*
(New York: Methuen, 1982); Suresh Raval, *Metacriticism* (Athens: University of Georgia Press, 1981); Henry Staten, *Wittgenstein and Derrida* (Lin-
coln: University of Nebraska Press, 1982).

meaning (that is, fixed, final, capitalized meaning) and its implications for the search for meaning, certitude, presence,
truth, or anything else one may care about. Therefore, it is
fair to say that the emphasis in what follows is on the deconstructing rather than the constructing, the undoing rather
than the preserving of meaning. It will become clear, I hope,
why deconstructionists present both parts of binary oppositions together (e.g., preserving/undoing), thus always presenting paradoxes.

Deconstruction is not so much a theory as it is a method of
critiquing theory. It therefore critiques, undercuts, deconstructs, and problematizes structural theory. Whereas structuralists have attempted to treat the structure of content, the
system of signs, anterior to all meaning, Derrida's project is to
treat the structurality of structure, the form/formlessness of
form, anterior to all signs. As we shall see, it is this that Derrida designates by his term "writing."

Derrida says that although structurality has always been at
work, it has been overlooked, neutralized, or reduced by assuming that there is within the structure a center, a presence,
a truth that governs, but is not itself, structurality. The center,
the truth, is the point at which the substitution of contents or
terms is no longer possible. This center organizes the structure but closes off the play of the structure it makes possible.[2]
Structuralists, for example, take meaning as a given, a center,
a point of reference, then try to identify the system of codes
responsible for the accepted meaning.

Derrida's project is to deconstruct this center, this meaning,
which he calls the transcendental signified—"transcendental"
because it is conceived of as a concept independent of language, an ideality exterior to the process of language, a something that language means to say. He identifies "logocentrism

---

[2] Derrida, *Writing and Difference*, trans. Alan Bass (Chicago: University
of Chicago Press, 1978), p. 278.

and the metaphysics of presence as the exigent, powerful, systematic, and irrepressible desire for such a signified,"[3] but says that "from the first texts I published I have attempted to systematize a deconstructive critique precisely against the authority of meaning, as the *transcendental signified* or as *telos*."[4] ("Telos" in Greek means completion of a cycle, consummation, perfection, finality.) In *Of Grammatology* Derrida says, that "to make enigmatic what one thinks one understands by the words 'proximity,' 'immediacy,' 'presence' . . . is my final intention."[5] Rather than seeing meaning as a center that governs structure, Derrida sees it as coming after, a product of, structurality.

As Derrida makes clear throughout *Of Grammatology*, "To affirm in this way that the concept of writing exceeds and comprehends that of language, presupposes of course a certain definition of language and of writing."[6] The science of writing, grammatology, is the "science of 'the arbitrariness of the sign,' science of the immotivation of the trace, science of writing before speech and in speech."[7] This science, according to Derrida, is the one Saussure staked out a place for, the one "Saussure saw without seeing, knew without being *able* to take into account,"[8] the one within which linguistics is only a part.[9] Because of the logocentrism within which "Saussure and the majority of his successors" worked, they were unable to see fully and explicitly what Derrida sees, that "writing

---

[3] Derrida, *Of Grammatology*, trans. Gayatri Spivak (Baltimore: Johns Hopkins University Press, 1974), p. 49.

[4] Derrida, *Positions*, trans. Alan Bass (Chicago: University of Chicago Press, 1981), p. 49.

[5] *Of Grammatology*, p. 70.

[6] Ibid., pp. 8–9.

[7] Ibid., p. 51.

[8] Ibid., p. 43.

[9] Derrida quotes the passage from the *Course in General Linguistics* (Bally and Sechehaye trans., p. 16) in which Saussure foretells a science of signs, but he substitutes the term "grammatology" for Saussure's "semiology." *Of Grammatology*, p. 51.

itself as the origin of language writes itself within Saussure's discourse."[10]

Derrida makes the point so often and explicitly himself that it seems hardly necessary here to point out that his grammatology is the working out of what is implicit in Saussure's definition of a sign. Yet this point is crucial because, as will become clear in the second part of this book, it is the dyadic character of the sign that prefigures the treatment of meaning in structuralism and deconstruction. Derrida accepts the Saussurean concepts of signifier/signified, *langue/parole*, and difference as essential and irreducible to the definition of language. In spite of his critique of Saussure's belief that "language and writing are two distinct systems of signs . . . the second [of which] exists for the sole purpose of representing the first"[11] and of the metaphysical baggage carried by Saussure's notion of a sign as signifier and signified, Derrida repeatedly makes statements such as the following:

> Of course, it is not a question of "rejecting" these notions; they are necessary and, at least at present, nothing is conceivable for us without them.[12]
>
> . . . .
>
> Since these concepts are indispensable for unsettling the heritage to which they belong, we should be even less prone to renounce them. . . . The concept of the sign is exemplary. We have just marked its metaphysical appurtenance.[13]

Saussure's definition of a sign is the means and justification of Derrida's deconstruction of meaning, truth, presence. The Saussurean notion of a sign is the "essential structure of the

---

[10] Derrida, *Of Grammatology*, pp. 43–44.

[11] Saussure, *Course in General Linguistics*, p. 23.

[12] Derrida, *Of Grammatology*, p. 13. See similar statements in his *Positions*, pp. 23–24.

[13] Derrida, *Of Grammatology*, p. 14.

sign" in Derrida's grammatology. His critique of history, reading, writing, and interpretation is predicated by it. Little wonder he repeatedly and explicitly reminds us that it would be "silly ... to dispose of the sign, of the term and the notion."[14] One finds this sentiment echoed in the works of other theorists as a key article of faith—the distinction Saussure makes in his definition of a sign is essential to any thought whatever. The important point being made here is that the Saussurean notion of a sign, even though Saussure's terms are put in question, problematized, and troped in the new universe of "writing" that they inspired, is for Derrida the "essential structure of the sign."

Derrida contends that the very concept of the arbitrary sign that signifies within a structure of oppositions and differences contains within it the necessity of language being "writing" prior to all speech and writing. This general "writing," as opposed to writing in the narrower sense of common usage, is the irreducible, anterior essence of all language that Derrida defines by the terms "trace," "differance," and "supplement." These terms expand or make explicit what is implicit in Saussure's concepts of the arbitrary nature of signs and of difference as the basis of all linguistic values and meanings.

Derrida's concept of "differance" is based on Saussure's statement that "in language there are only differences *without positive terms.*"[15] Assuming language to be anterior to all history, knowledge, and experience, he arrives at his deconstructive critique by focusing on the form of form.[16] More basic than signifier or signified is this form/formlessness of language which Derrida calls "differance" and "trace"—and sometimes calls "nothing" because it is *no thing.* It is the character of language as differance that simultaneously defers presence and enables signification. Because of this essential

[14] Ibid.
[15] Saussure, *Course in General Linguistics*, p. 120.
[16] Staten, *Wittgenstein and Derrida*, p. 13.

structure of difference, what seems to *be* only *seems* to be. What seems to *be* is already signs of signs, but the supplementary character of these signs goes unnoticed. Between the signifier and the signified, the word and the thing, the statement and the meaning, the expression and what is expressed, the representer and the represented, is the space, the gap, where the thing signified is lost in order to be signified.

Derrida defines the "instituted trace" as the unmotivated character of a signifier, the arbitrariness of a sign, the sign as sign, the sign as difference within a structure of differences that makes it possible for any oppositions to have meaning. It is the "possible" character of the signifier that allows it to have a signified. It marks the rupture of the seemingly "natural attachment" of the signifier to the signified in reality. It is the becoming-unmotivated character of signs, the becoming-sign of the symbol. With this term and notion Derrida stresses what is implied in Saussure's concept of the arbitrary nature of signs: in language there are no foundations and no signifieds other than signs of signs. "All begins with the trace," and "there is above all no originary trace."[17] The trace is *nothing* (no thing) and therefore cannot be treated as an object. Trace is not present—only its path among possibilities which signifies that the origin of the signifier and the signified is *nothing*. These statements are particularly enigmatic when lifted out of the contexts of Derrida's fuller treatment of them, but Derrida's point is that in language there are no essences, identities, or even signs that present themselves as such. There is no origin of sense except the trace or differ*a*nce that makes signs iterable and makes them differ from and defer that which they represent. The signifier is always already a signified, and the signified is always already a signifier; in the final analysis, one has only a sign of a sign which is for Derrida a *supplement* that not only adds itself to and replaces what it represents but

[17] Derrida, *Of Grammatology*, p. 61.

that also effaces its supplementary role. In language, and hence in experience, everything (including meaning, being, presence) is always already a sign of a sign in a system of signs, that is, *absent*.

It is not simply that signs put reality at one remove or at two or three removes. It is not only because signs "represent" the real that we do not experience the presence of the thing itself. Rather, Derrida says, in our experience there never was a real. The belief that there was a reality is the illusion on which we construct our metaphysical notions of presence, origin, truth. There is *nothing* real behind the sign "mother" for Rousseau, not only because his mother died in giving birth to him but because the only origin of "mother" is a trace, which is to say there is no origin, no point at which "mother" is anything other than a sign of a sign. No matter how far back one may search to find the origin, the presence, the real thing that the word "mother" originally represents, one will still find nothing but the supplement that adds to and replaces another supplement. "The absolute present, Nature, that which words like 'real mother' name, have always already escaped, have never existed; ... what opens meaning and language is writing as the disappearance of natural presence."[18] Or, to put the case in positive terms, "only a form is *self-evident*, only a form has or is an *essence*, only a form *presents itself* a such."[19]

Writing, which Derrida says will appear to us more and more as another name for supplementarity, "makes possible all that constitutes the property of man: speech, society, passion, etc."[20] Moreover, this supplementarity makes man possible:

---

[18] Ibid., p. 159.

[19] Derrida, *Margins of Philosophy*, trans. Alan Bass (Chicago: University of Chicago Press, 1982), pp. 157–158.

[20] Derrida, *Of Grammatology*, p. 244.

On the one hand, [supplementarity] is that of which the possibility must be thought before man, and outside of him. Man allows himself to be announced to himself after the fact of supplementarity, which is thus not an attribute—accidental or essential—of man. For on the other hand, supplementarity, which *is nothing*, neither a presence nor an absence, is neither a substance nor an essence of man. It is precisely the play of presence and absence, the opening of this play that no metaphysical or ontological concept can comprehend. Therefore this property [*propre*] of man is not a property of man: it is the very dislocation of the proper in general: it is the dislocation of the characteristic, the proper in general, the impossibility—and therefore the desire—of self-proximity; the impossibility and therefore the desire of pure presence.... [The play of supplementarity] precedes what one calls man and extends outside of him. Man *calls himself* man only by drawing limits excluding his other from the play of supplementarity: the purity of nature, of animality, primitivism, childhood, madness, divinity. The approach to these limits is at once feared as a threat of death, and desired as access to a life without differance. The history of man *calling himself* man is the articulation of *all* these limits among themselves. All concepts determining a non-supplementarity (Nature, animality, primitivism, childhood, madness, divinity, etc.) have evidently no truth-value. They belong—moreover, with the idea of truth itself—to an epoch of supplementarity. They have meaning only within a closure of the game.[21]

Derrida's thesis is that the origin and essence of everything to which we attribute substance is "writing." Even the sounds of spoken signifiers and the contents of intelligible signifieds

[21] Ibid., pp. 244–245.

are supplements of supplements made possible by the play of *differance*, by the trace that is *nothing*; that is, they are not essences present to consciousness but are always already blanks, spaces, gaps between the signifiers and the signifieds—anterior to all signs, making signs possible. Therefore, there can be no science conceivable to study them. Phonology, the equation of signs with sounds, and semantics, the equation of signs with meanings, ignore the primordial nature of language as "writing." According to Derrida they are efforts to close the possibilities of trace, to stop the movement of *differance*, to make meaning seem natural and inevitable, rather than accidental and possible. The repression of the play of difference is for Derrida always a premature and tentative, perhaps political and repressive, act of "closure," yielding the illusion that presence and meaning are antecedent to, more original than, outside of *differance*—a repression that is, of course, blind to its own self-deception.

Much, perhaps most, of Derrida's deconstructive effort has gone into shaking us out of the belief that we have full intentional presence to the "contents" of signs in conscious thought. In trying to communicate the implications of his concept of language as writing, he is forced into statements that seem to be paradoxical or self-contradictory. Consequently, his commentary frequently runs something like this: what is present in any given instant is nothing; what is essential in language to make essence thinkable is the accidental. His insistence on the priority of "deferral," "absence," "nothing," "gap," "space," "outside," etc. reverses their hierarchical positions in the oppositions in which he finds them, risks sounding like nonsense, and falls prey to the ineluctable trap of ideality that it is attempting to expose and that (according to his analysis) all *use* of language must fall prey to.

This deconstruction, by stretching terms such as "presence" and "essence" "to include what they were expressly designed to exclude,"[22] by tying them irreducibly to what is a denial of them, forces us to shift our focus from our logocentric associations with these terms to differ*a*nce. If, after having arrived at an understanding of Derrida's concept of language as "writing," as trace, differ*a*nce, supplementarity, we fall back into our habit of logocentric and metaphysical thought, we may very easily arrive at a metaphysics of nihilism. This is particularly true of those who read Derrida's work looking for a consistent system or theory. Suresh Raval[23] and others who find Derrida's project of deconstruction to be a metaphysics of nihilism maintain that Derrida's *nothing* is *something*; his *always already absent* is *present*; his position is always already what it opposes—hence a metaphysics of antimetaphysics.

Derrideans wince at the charge of being metaphysical, protesting that the charge could not even be made unless one totally misunderstood the concept of the deconstruction of the transcendental signified. Anyone, they say, who understands Derrida's concept of "writing" should recognize that metaphysics and nihilism are two sides of the same coin, and that deconstruction undercuts both. It is not, then, Derrida's project of deconstruction, but the logocentric reading of his concepts, that is "metaphysical."

For his part, Derrida fully anticipated both sides of this argument. There are, he said, "two interpretations of interpretation, of structure, of sign, of play." The one will seek truth and an origin that escapes play; it will be the saddened, negative view that focuses on "the lost or impossible presence of the absent origin." The other is "the joyous affirmation of the play of the world and of the innocence of becoming, the affirmation of a world of signs without fault, without truth,

---

[22] Staten, *Wittgenstein and Derrida*, p. 53.
[23] *Metacriticism*, pp. 209–238.

and without origin which is offered to an active interpretation."[24]

There is a sense, of course, in which Derrida's project of deconstruction cannot be wholly vindicated of the charge of being metaphysical. As Derrida says repeatedly, even if one believes in the endless possibility of interpretation, any particular interpretation, all *use* of language (including Derrida's), involves ideality. Even though what is forever absent according to Derrida's conception of *langue* is the object, or the objectified, his notion of the free play of differ*a*nce in a system without a center (object) is a center related only to the formal system. I think it is fair to say of Derrida that while he puts in question presence, essence, and ideality, his project is itself an attempt to get at what is most fundamental to language, yes, what is immanent to language. However one characterizes it, Derrida's finding is that prior to any conception of meaning or presence derived from signs is the arbitrary trace, the play of differ*a*nce, the supplementary supplement, the nothing (trace) on which the conception is based, the "writing" that opens up signs to a nonpresence, a not-here, a not-now which make meaning possible but do not determine it.

His conception of writing as the primordial basis of all linguistic and cultural activity *and* as the dangerous knowledge that culture must repress serves Derrida in a number of ways. First, it functions for Derrida just as the concept of the autonomy of literature functioned for the New Critics. The doctrine of the autonomous text liberated the New Critics from the control of authors' intentions and genetic considerations and gave the appearance of objectivity to their interpretations. What is autonomous for Derrida is a very complex language characterized by its writtenness; that is, by the play of trace and supplement that defers meaning endlessly. This autonomous language system "opens" meaning but never "fixes" it.

[24] Derrida, *Writing and Difference*, p. 292.

Hence, the interpreter of language is freed from everything but the play of difference that he or she discovers in the text.

Second, Derrida's conception of writing functions as an interpretive strategy for reading literature, philosophy, and theology; it takes the binary oppositions he finds described (if not declared) *in the text*, shows that one term of the opposition has been hierarchically subordinated to the other, reverses the hierarchical positions of the terms, and then shows the mutual dependence and interpenetration of the opposites. What he always finds is that "something which was never spoken and which is nothing other than writing itself as the origin of language writes itself within Saussure's [or Lévi-Strauss's or Rousseau's or Husserl's] discourse."[25] Consequently, the texts Derrida reads never mean what they say or say what they mean, but always mean more than they say and often the opposite of what they say.

Third, Derrida's conception of writing gives the "final no" to meaning. After making reference to Husserl's distinction between *Sinn* ("All experience is the experience of meaning. . . . Everything that appears to consciousness, everything that is for consciousness in general, is *meaning*")[26] and *Bedeutung* (meaning as signification, meaning something, meaning at the conceptual level), Derrida says that in both conceptions of meaning, whether meaning is thought of as "signified" or "expressed," " 'meaning' is an intelligible or spiritual *ideality* which eventually can be united to the sensible aspect of the signifier that in itself it does not need."[27] Derrida goes to great lengths to deconstruct any interpretation that subordinates "the movement of *differance* in favor of the presence of a value or a meaning supposedly antecedent to *differance*, more original than it, exceeding and governing it in the last analysis."[28]

[25] Derrida, *Of Grammatology*, p. 44.
[26] Derrida, *Positions*, p. 30.
[27] Ibid., p. 31.
[28] Ibid., p. 28.

Such operations make meaning a "transcendental signified," a concept independent of language, an ideality exterior to the process of language, a something language means to say. Language as writing means to say nothing. There is nothing in the system of differance that *means to say.* "Wherever it operates, 'thought' means nothing."[29] "The play of *differance* ... prevents any word, any concept, any major enunciation from coming to summarize and to govern from the theological presence of a center the movement and textual spacing of differences."[30]

Nowhere does it become more clear what the implications of language as writing are for meaning than in Derrida's analysis of the speech-act theory of J. L. Austin. In "Signature Event Context"[31] Derrida shows that since meaning is bound by and dependent on context, it is not limited by intention of the speaker. But since possible contexts are limitless and no context can be "saturated," meaning cannot be controlled or limited. Hence one cannot appeal to intention or context for an authoritative determination of meaning. Derrida's conclusion about meaning, then, is that it is an effect of differance, not its cause or master. It is infinitely possible but grounded in differance, that is, *nothing.* Of course, meaning is grounded in context, in syntax, in language, but since these are as variable as differance, we come back to the same conclusion.

The problem is not that Derrida makes it impossible to talk meaningfully about meaning. Commentary on meaning pervades all of Derrida's work and is inseparable from his treatment of essence, concept, and history. To use Derrida's term, deconstruction "opens" meaning by making it infinitely possible, which of course involves making context infinitely var-

---

[29] Ibid., p. 49.
[30] Ibid., p. 14.
[31] Derrida, *Margins of Philosophy*, pp. 307–330. Also translated by Samuel Weber and Jeffrey Mehlman in *Glyph: Johns Hopkins Textual Studies* 7 (1977).

iable. We have not lost meaning, but meaning has lost its value. We do not value any particular meaning because we have become convinced that we are dealing in a system of pure symbol, pure form, pure law, pure abstraction, pure nothing. In such a system anything is possible. Where everything is possible, nothing is of particular value.

Since language is pure form and human users have no place "in" language, intention, meaning to say, and validity of interpretation are "outside" of it. Consequently, language, not the users (individually or as a community), is the final authority on meaning. Since language intends to say nothing, it opens the play of differance, always means more than any particular human writer or thinker, and judges any understandings or interpretations to be premature closures of the play of differences. The only interpretations that escape being premature closures are those that show the universal (the play of differance) in the particular. Like structuralism, deconstruction values the particular only as a manifestation of a general universal structure.

To speak of meaning as endlessly possible is, of course, to speak of endless possibilities of closure that would in each case be blind to the deferral of meaning—that is, blind to language as writing. Derrida finds in language an "irreducible structure of 'deferral' in its relationships to consciousness, presence, science, history."[32] Any theory based on differance can never escape the "deferral," "absence," and "blindness" that undercut any effort to treat determinate meaning. Perhaps this explains why, as Jonathan Culler has pointed out, "Derrida frequently writes about literary works but has not dealt directly with topics such as the task of literary criticism, the methods of analyzing literary language, or the nature of literary meaning."[33] Within a system of differance, meaning appears as an

---

[32] Derrida, *Positions*, p. 5.
[33] Culler, *On Deconstruction*, p. 180.

ideality, exterior to the process of language; and to try to treat meaning is to fall prey to the ineluctable logocentrism and metaphysics of presence that deconstruction sets out to critique.

According to Derrida, the birth and death, the source and denial of meaning are one and the same—writing. Writing deconstitutes what it institutes, undermines what it shapes, dislocates what it constructs, creates the desire for the thing it forbids, makes impossible the very thing it makes possible. Forget those misguided efforts to discover ontological-theological truth. The search for presence, being, truth is a fool's errand, a quixotic quest. Meaning cannot be treated as such any more than can essence or presence.

Derrida's deconstruction, as he himself claims, is already implied in the antitheses within which he works out his theory. The dyadic character of the sign that makes oppositions irreducible and makes everything in opposition mutually dependent on each other for meaning makes inevitable the conclusion that every sign is always already a sign of its relation to its other. Or, one could say, its irreducible relationship to its other makes it a sign. That is why *Of Grammatology* is filled with statements such as the signifier is always already the signified, presence is always already absence, reality is always already a sign. But even such statements involve what Derrida calls closure. Between the poles of closure is the "becoming," the "relating to," the "play of differance" that is always absent *and* the source and deferral of meaning. Consequently, in every sign, word, event, or text is the "mysterious absence," the "always-interpretable-but-never-closed gap"[34] that is the source and deferral of meaning but eludes observation and scrutiny. It is what never becomes a sign itself.

Both structuralism and deconstruction are theories of the

---

[34] Eric Gould, *Mythical Intentions in Modern Literature* (Princeton: Princeton University Press, 1981), p. 175.

"gap" inherent in the dyadic conception of the sign. The principal difference between the two is that the first tries to account for what fills the gap, what structures are in place, whereas the second maintains that no conceivable science or ontology can study the movement of the trace within the gap. Structuralists say that there are structures and codes and myths operating in the gap between signifier and signified, sign and meaning, writer's mind and writer's words, understanding and interpretation. They claim to tell *how* texts mean, but not *what*. Any meaning arises in the relation between the text and the "intermediaries" operating in the gap. Deconstructionists say that the play of trace, differ*a*nce, within the gap defers meaning endlessly. Without the retention of differ*a*nce, not only between but also within signs, no meaning can arise; because of such retention of differ*a*nce, the gap is irreducible and meaning is deferred. This ambivalent function of the gap leads to the "preserving/undoing" arguments of the deconstructionists. Any meaning or identity is an ideality that denies the constant motion of signs. Both structuralism and deconstruction lose the ability to talk with any conviction about "the meaning of *something*" because of the gap inherent in the dyadic sign.

Even if we disagree with the deconstructionists' conclusions about meaning, it is not fruitful to point out, as many have, the contradiction between deconstruction's praxis and theory. To do so within the Saussurean-Derridean conception of language leads nowhere, and we find ourselves caught up in the very web we set out to critique. Even though we can show that deconstructionists' principles undercut the certainty of their own theories, paradoxically that seems to confirm rather than deny their accuracy, for what they assert is the impossibility of determinate, authoritative meaning. Moreover, deconstructive thought would encourage yet undermine our critique of deconstruction. Paul de Man, in his *Blindness and Insight*, explains that while capable of detecting the blindness of prior readings, every interpretation, including his own and any we might make, is "caught in its own form of blindness."[35] Blindness is not a defect to be remedied, but a universal characteristic of all human action that enables insight but marks it as "possible," "partial," "premature closure."

Therefore, I do not propose to refute or add to the treatment of meaning *within* the Saussurean "science of signs." However, there is another place, another definition of the sign, from which we can begin building language and literary theory. Charles Peirce's definition of the sign as triadic has not been totally ignored by literary theorists, but it has almost always been translated into Saussurean, dyadic terms. In Part Two of this book we will incorporate much of what has been learned through the study of the dyadic sign into a Peircean theory of language based on a triadic sign. There we will see that Peirce's theory of signs allows us to create a theory of interpretation that is just as logically rigorous and intellectually satisfying as structural and poststructural theory, but that makes it possible to find meaning *in* signs, texts, events. Peirce's theory of signs does not deny that "from the moment that there is meaning there are nothing but signs,"[36] but his definition of a sign does not separate the mind made world from the "real" world *in* which we live and move and *have being*.

The dyadic sign is a remnant of classical Western thinking, which assumes that to study things as they "really are" is to study them as external, autonomous, isolated objects, to see everything as parts and wholes. Such a mindset is behind Lévi-Strauss's assertion that "the goal of the human sciences is not to constitute man but to dissolve him."[37] The humani-

---

[35] De Man, *Blindness and Insight: Essays in the Rhetoric of Contemporary Criticism* (New York: Oxford University Press, 1971), p. 139.

[36] Derrida, *Of Grammatology*, p. 50.

[37] Claude Lévi-Strauss, *La Pensée sauvage* (Paris: Plon, 1962), p. 326; cited

ties and arts, on the other hand, have always worked from *within* the context of the human experience of trying to come to terms with objects and relations. Stories, pictures, and histories have served to illuminate the "relating" of humans to their environments.[38] Structural and poststructural theory, however, has caused us to lose faith in both our analysis and our experience of art and life, which is the same as to say that we lose faith in our ability to discover and assign determinable meaning. Peirce's theory of signs incorporates the human user into the sign. Therefore, signs are not independent of human users, of intention, of meaning to say, of valid interpretations.

Culler, Fish, Todorov, Barthes, Eco, Iser, Derrida, and others treated in the foregoing chapters have perceptively explored the implications for literary study of the conception of a dyadic sign, which for them is *the* sign. Derrida, however, demonstrates convincingly and repeatedly that so long as we have a conception of language that begins with Saussure's dyadic sign, meaning cannot be treated *as such* any more than can essence or presence. Given the strength of his conclusions, it is somewhat puzzling why more people have not questioned the necessity of starting with Saussure. Derrida, although he makes a case for starting with Saussure, admits that the choice of where we begin is just that, a choice, a nonrational act: "the thought of the trace . . . has already taught us that it is impos-

---

in Jonathan Culler, *The Pursuit of Signs* (London: Routledge & Kegan Paul, 1981), p. 33.

[38] I think that much of the "experimental fiction" of such writers as John Barth, Thomas Pynchon, Robert Coover, Donald Barthelme, and Vladimir Nabokov portrays experiences of people for whom reality is endlessly displaced by fiction, and truth by fabulation and deception. By giving multiple accounts of the same events, and by constantly shifting without warning from one level of fiction to another, these works portray what it is like to be unable to assume, pretend, or believe in any "fiction" as "real." Robert Scholes has said that "what Barth, Pynchon, and Coover have tried to give us in [their] books is nothing less than the kind of realism this culture deserves" (*Fabulation and Metafiction* [Urbana: University of Illinois Press, 1979], p. 209).

sible to justify a point of departure absolutely."[39] Structural and poststructural literary theorists begin with a dyadic sign. The hallmark of their thought is that everything is always beyond the scope of their theory because it is not accounted for in the dyadic and arbitrary sign. Structuralist and post-structuralist thought reflects (perhaps causes) a swing in modern scholarship from a stance of theoretical certainty to theoretical uncertainty. Literary studies as a discipline are doubtlessly undergoing change because of these influences. It is within this milieu that the sign theory of Charles Peirce can give us a genuinely new opening to many of the old questions about autonomy, intention, validity of interpretation, the meaning of meaning.

[39] Derrida, *Of Grammatology*, p. 162.

PART TWO

$\triangledown$

Meaning Is a Triadic Relation

Not words of routine this song of mine,
But abruptly to question, to leap beyond yet nearer
    bring;
This printed and bound book—but the printer
    and the printing-office boy?
The well-taken photographs—but your wife or
    friend close and solid in your arms?
. . . .

The saints and sages in history—but you yourself?
Sermons, creeds, theology—but the fathomless
    human brain,
And what is reason? and what is love? and what is
    life?

        —Walt Whitman, "Song of Myself"

FOUR

Starting Over:
Peirce's Theory of Signs

Now a definition does not reveal the Object of a
Sign, its Denotation, but only analyzes its Signification, and *that* is a question not of the sign's relation to its Object but of its relation to its Interpretant.

—Charles S. Peirce's Letters to Lady Welby

The nemesis of human understanding in literary theory based
on the Saussurean sign, as shown in the preceding chapters, is
the gap between the signifier and the signified, the word and
what it represents, the statement and its meaning. If one has
nothing but systems of dyadic signs whose parts have no logical, natural, or motivated relation, one is left with mystifica-
tion and blindness when one tries to define the meaning of a
sign. The definition or meaning of the signified is not determined by its signifier but by something else. Structuralists call
this "something else" differences with other signs in the system. None of the signs *have* meaning in themselves; rather,
the differences between (and within) signs *allow* meaning.
Consequently, as Derrida has shown so thoroughly, all meaning is supplementarity, an ideality exterior to the process of
language.

There are other theories of interpretation that reject the
dyadic sign and its replication in various subject/object dual-

isms. Examples of other approaches to interpretation that reject the dyadic, objectivist presuppositions are the philosophical hermeneutics of Martin Heidegger and Hans-Georg Gadamer and the language theory of Ludwig Wittgenstein. These are often studied from a "Saussurean" perspective and therefore end up looking metaphysical (e.g., Derrida's treatment of Heidegger) or supportive of structural theory (e.g., positivistic interpretations of Wittgenstein). In order to appreciate fully the alternative that their philosophies of "grounds" (modes of meaning) offer to the structural theory of "gaps" (the theoretical absence of meaning), we need a theory of signs that can relate phenomenology and ontology, modes of consciousness and modes of being. Such a theory of signs was developed by Saussure's American contemporary Charles Sanders Peirce. Peirce's "semiotic," or "doctrine of signs," provides a new starting point, an alternative frame of reference, that allows semioticians, all interpreters of signs in every field of study, to see beyond the limitations set by Saussure's analysis of the sign and clarifies many of the issues that have been problematic in the understanding and interpretation of literature.

In order to show how Peirce's theory clarifies these issues, it is first necessary to introduce the terms and concepts fundamental to Peirce's theory of signs. Peirce describes his semiotic as "Logic, in its general sense," as "the quasi-necessary, or formal, doctrine of signs" (2.227).[1] He does not assume a

[1] The Collected Papers of Charles Sanders Peirce, vols. 1–6, ed. Charles Hartshorne and Paul Weiss, 1931–1935; vols. 7–8, ed. A. W. Burks, 1958 (Cambridge: Harvard University Press). All further references to The Collected Papers are parenthesized within the body of the text; the first numeral in such references is the volume number, and the number to the right of the point is the paragraph.

A new edition of Peirce's writings is currently being published by Indiana University Press. Volume 1 of Writings of Charles S. Peirce: A Chronological Edition came out in 1982 and includes materials from Peirce's very

privileged position of objectivity outside of language or human consciousness. By a process he calls abstractive observation, "which is at bottom very much like mathematical reasoning," he gives us a theory of "what *must be* the character of all signs used by a 'scientific' intelligence, that is to say, by an intelligence capable of learning by experience" (2.227). Peirce worked on his theory over a period of several decades and had not yet completed it to his own satisfaction when he died. But the aspects of his theory that are most important to the present discussion, that is, his definition of a sign and its relation to his categories, remained fundamentally unchanged during Peirce's lifetime.

A SIGN

Peirce was at least half serious when he said that philosophy would do well "to provide itself with a vocabulary so outlandish that loose thinkers shall not be tempted to borrow its words" (2.223). In reading the next few pages, which define the basic terms and concepts of Peirce's semiotic, the reader may well come to believe that Peirce took his own advice. I will follow one of Peirce's less troublesome practices and risk repetition in order to make these terms and concepts clear.

The concept most fundamental to Peirce's theory is that of a sign. Peirce defines a sign as follows:

---

early years, 1857–1866. Volume 2 came out in 1984, and volume 3 in 1986. This new edition is valuable primarily because of the chronological ordering of material and the prefatory historical and biographical information in each volume. Since the aspects of Peirce's theory that are most important to the present book (his definition of a sign and its relation to his categories) are ones that remained fundamentally unchanged during his lifetime, almost all the writings of Peirce to which I refer explicitly were written after 1893. Since volume 3 of the new Peirce project contains writings only as far as the year 1878, I cite *The Collected Papers of Charles Sanders Peirce* exclusively.

A sign or *representamen*, is something which stands to somebody for something in some respect or capacity. It addresses somebody, that is creates in the mind of that person an equivalent sign, or perhaps a more developed sign. That sign which it creates I call the *interpretant* of the first sign. The sign stands for something, its *object*. It stands for that object, not in all respects, but in reference to a sort of idea, which I have sometimes called the *ground* of the representamen. [2.228]

An understanding of the italicized terms is essential. Probably the most ambiguous term is "ground." Peirce says that "every representamen" is "connected with three things, the ground, the object, and the interpretant" (2.229). Moreover, he says that the branch of semiotics dealing with "ground" is "*pure grammar*," whose task is "to ascertain what must be true of the representamen used by every scientific intelligence in order that they may embody any *meaning*" (2.229).

Peirce's immediate concern in the context in which we find the above definition is to inquire into the character of signs themselves. But in a later essay entitled "Meaning" (1910) Peirce enlarges upon the idea of "ground." He says, "If a Sign is other than its Object, there must exist, either in thought or expression, some explanation or argument or other context, showing how—upon what system or for what reason the Sign represents the Object or set of Objects that it does" (2.230). The "ground," which Peirce in the above quotations makes synonymous with "a sort of idea" and "some explanation or argument," turns out to be nothing more nor less than the context or language game within which the sign relates to its interpretant. "The peculiarity of it [a sign], therefore, lies in its mode of meaning; and to say this is to say that its peculiarity lies in its relation to its interpretant" (2.252).

Peirce, near the end of his life, wrote in a letter to Lady

Welby: "Now a definition does not reveal the Object of a Sign, its Denotation, but only analyzes its Signification, and *that* is a question not of the sign's relation to its Object but of its relation to its Interpretant."[2] If Peirce had tried to put his finger on the weakness of Saussure's definition of a sign (and hence upon the weakness of structural and poststructural literary theory), he could not have done it better than with this statement. What Saussure's definition of a sign does *not* account for is that which determines the sign's meaning, the relation of the sign's object or signified to its interpretant. Saussure and his followers, recognizing that a signifier does not determine the signified's meaning, but at the same time trying to establish the autonomy of the language as a system, designate what is missing as an unbridgeable gap in the system. As I will show in some detail, Peirce gives us a definition of a sign that adds to the sign/object, signifier/signified relationship the interpretant, a sign in the mind, and he argues that this triadic relation is irreducible and always has meaning.[3] In fact, meaning is the medium, the mediator, the

---

[2] 14 March 1909, *Charles S. Peirce's Letters to Lady Welby*, ed. Irwin C. Lieb (New Haven, Conn.: Whitlocks, 1953), p. 39.

[3] Some may wonder whether Derrida's "differance" might be seen as a third element in the sign comparable to Peirce's "interpretant." For example, G. Douglas Atkins, noting J. Hillis Miller's explicit statement in the "Critic as Host" that in binary oppositions "the relation is a triangle, not a polar opposition," suggests that "the 'trace' may be this 'third' " (*Reading Deconstruction, Deconstructive Reading* [Lexington: University of Kentucky Press, 1983], p. 81). I have no quarrel with either Miller or Atkins about their conclusions, but it is important not to get confused and think that the ability to speak of a "triangle" or a "third" in binary oppositions erases the limitations of the dyadic sign or makes it somehow triadic. We have seen in the above pages that to speak of sign/object/interpretant in triadic *relation* is to imply what may be thought of as a fourth component. A sign (*representamen*) stands to somebody (creates *interpretant*) for something (its *object*) "in some respect or capacity" (the *ground*) (2.228). To speak of *the relation* in a dyadic or triadic relation as a third or fourth component is a redundancy. The main point here is that Derrida's trace or differance is not the

ground by which we experience sign/object relations. In light of the recognized but theoretically essential lack in the Saussurean sign, it is understandable that structuralists have not only been unable to generate and evaluate interpretations of texts, but have seen interpretations as suppressions of the play of language, as blindness to the perpetual oscillations of meaning in the system of difference. Moreover, the mindset that divides the sign into arbitrary signifiers and signifieds leads to a misunderstanding of Wittgenstein's linguistic turn, a concept that has numerous implications for semiotics of literature, particularly in relation to reader-response theory.

Other of Peirce's definitions of a sign describe not only the triadic relation within which a sign must be embodied in order to signify, but also the generation of signs and the modes of being that signs represent. In Baldwin's *Dictionary of Philosophy and Psychology* (1902) Peirce defined a sign as "anything which determines something else (its *interpretant*) to refer to an object to which itself refers (its *object*) in the same way, the interpretant becoming in turn a sign, and so on *ad infinitum*" (2.303). And in his unpublished "Syllabus," written about the same time as the above definition, Peirce states:

> A *Sign*, or *Representamen*, is a First which stands in such a genuine triadic relation to a Second, called its *Object*, as to be capable of determining a Third, called its *Interpretant*, to assume the same triadic relation to its Object in which it stands itself to the same Object. The triadic

---

equivalent of Peirce's interpretant. However, differ*a*nce has a similar (not the same) function in the dyadic sign that the ground has in the triadic sign. Both are necessary for there to be any relation, any meaning at all. So long as one stays within the tradition of "difference," the "third" (in the sense of Miller's and Atkins's statements) will always be a gap, no-thing. In a later chapter I will discuss some parallels between the theories of Derrida and Peirce.

relation is *genuine*, that is its three members are bound together by it in a way that does not consist in any complexus of dyadic relations. . . . The Third . . . must have a second triadic relation in which the Representamen, or rather the relation thereof to its Object, shall be its own (the Third's) Object, and must be capable of determining a Third to this relation. All this must equally be true of the Third's Third and so on endlessly. [2.274]

The triadic relation described in the first definition of a sign quoted above may be visualized thus:

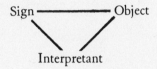

In the last statement quoted above, Peirce inserts First, Second, and Third. I will treat these concepts in the next few pages, but to avoid confusion later on it is important to emphasize immediately that Peirce is saying here that the triadic sign partakes of each of his three trichotomies, not each of his three modes of being. In other words, he is simply saying that the triadic relation of sign-object-interpretant is the irreducible character of any sign that signifies. The reader may wish to return to the above quotation after studying the chart showing Peirce's categories, later in this chapter. Peirce says in the last two definitions quoted above that the interpretant must be able to cause a second triadic connection in which the relation-of-the-sign-to-its-object in the first triad becomes the object of the interpretant (which assumes the position of a sign, that is, representamen, in the new triad). The following schematic may be helpful in visualizing the process of how an

interpretant of a sign in a sign-object-interpretant relation becomes a sign in a new triadic relation, and so on:

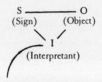

The relation-of-the-sign-to-its-object in the first triad becomes the object of the interpretant, which assumes the position of a sign in a new triad:

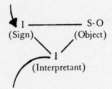

"And so on endlessly":

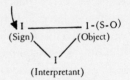

"[A]nd this, and more, is involved in the familiar idea of a
Sign; and as the term Representamen is here used, nothing
more is implied" (2.274).

My rather simplistic diagram helps us to see what is involved in the generative nature of signs. First of all, we see
the increasing complexity of the object: "A sign may have
more than one Object. Thus, the sentence 'Cain killed Abel,'
which is a Sign, refers at least as much to Abel as to Cain,
even if it be not regarded as it should, as having 'a killing' as
a third Object. But the set of Objects may be regarded as mak-

ing up one complex Object" (2.230). Furthermore, we can understand why Peirce's definition of object is so encompassing:

> The Objects—for a sign may have any number of them—may each be a single known existing thing or thing believed formerly to have existed or expected to exist, or a collection of such things, or a known quality or relation or fact, which single Object may be a collection, or whole of parts, or it may have some other mode of being, such as some act permitted whose being does not prevent its negation from being equally permitted, or something of a general nature desired, required, or invariably found under certain general circumstances. [2.232]

Any sign or collection of signs that a person has experienced in the past can become an object in the representamen-object-interpretant relationship that allows signs to be represented, that is, to have meaning.

Second, a sign functioning as a representamen, whether it is a thought or a feeling, is a First to the degree that it is immediately present. A representamen can be no more than an "absolutely simple and unanalyzable" feeling, "a mere sensation without parts," "simply an ultimate, inexplicable fact" (5.289). "Whenever we think," Peirce says, "we have present to the consciousness some feeling, image, conception or other representation, which serves as a sign ... *to* some thought which interprets it" (5.283). Every sign is interpreted by a subsequent sign or thought in which the relation-of-the-sign-to-its-object becomes the object of the new sign.

Not only does a sign *refer to* a subsequent thought-sign that interprets it, it also stands *for* some object through a previous thought-sign. The only way a sign can stand for any object, regardless of how complex or artificial, is by referring to it through previous thought. Since we are conscious only of previous thoughts, immediate consciousness of signs is not possi-

ble. The implications of these ideas will be developed in subsequent chapters; the present effort is simply to give a brief
account of Peirce's theory of signs.

That theory is merely an elaboration of his definition of a
sign, and his trichotomies and classes of signs make no sense
and have no validity unless viewed in the light of this definition of a sign. Peirce's method is to reason "from the definition of a Sign what sort of thing *ought* to be noticeable and
then searching for its appearance."[4]

THE CATEGORIES

Firstness, Secondness, and Thirdness, as the above discussion
of signs implies, are central to Peirce's classification of signs.
In fact, the three categories are the basis on which Peirce attempts "to outline a theory so comprehensive that, for a long
time to come, the entire work of human reason, in philosophy
of every school and kind, in mathematics, in psychology, in
physical science, in history, in sociology, and in whatever
other department there may be, shall appear as the filling up
of its details" (1.1). Hence, definitions and examples of these
three categories abound in Peirce's papers, in at least as many
different contexts as there are disciplines in the above quotation. For example, Peirce says that in logic and philosophy
three conceptions perpetually turn up, conceptions he calls
First, Second, Third: "First," he says, "is the conception of
being or existing independent of anything else. Second is the
conception of being relative to, the conception of reaction
with, something else. Third is the conception of mediation,
whereby the first and second are brought into relation" (6.32).
And when Peirce is writing a refutation of nominalism, he
states:

[4] 14 March 1909, *Letters to Lady Welby*, p. 36.

My view is that there are three modes of being. I hold that we can directly observe them in elements of whatever is at any time before the mind in any way. They are the being of positive qualitative possibility [Firstness], the being of actual fact [Secondness], and the being of law that will govern facts in the future [Thirdness]. [1.23]

Firstness is the mode of being that consists in something being what it is without reference to anything else. "That," Peirce says, "can only be a possibility" (1.25). The qualities of phenomena have such being. "The mode of being a *redness*, before anything in the universe was yet red, was nevertheless a positive qualitative possibility. And redness in itself, even if it be embodied, is something positive and *sui generis*. That I call Firstness" (1.25). The Qualisign (a quality that is a sign), we shall see in subsequent pages, is nothing but Firstness. Secondness is the being of actual fact:

> The actuality of the event seems to lie in its relation to the universe of existents. . . . Actuality is something brute. There is no reason for it. I instance putting your shoulder against a door and trying to force it open against an unseen, silent and unknown resistance. We have a two-sided consciousness of effort and resistance, which seems to me to come tolerably near to a pure sense of actuality. . . . I call that Secondness. [1.24]

This category of fact, of individual existence with its binarity and bruteness (absence of reason, regularity, and rule; that is, Thirdness) is dyadic (2.84). Thirdness, as a category of being, consists in that tendency of things to take habits, to come together in such a way as to be predictable, "to conform to a general rule" (1.26).

Perhaps the most helpful treatment of the categories for a

study of signs is Peirce's treatment of these categories in consciousness:

> It seems, then, that the true categories of consciousness are: first, feeling, the consciousness which can be included with an instant of time, passive consciousness of quality, without recognition or analysis; second, consciousness of an interruption into the field of consciousness, sense of resistance, of an external fact, or another something; third, synthetic consciousness, binding time together, sense of learning, thought. [1.377]

A feeling is "a quality of immediate consciousness" (1.307). It is not an event—which would be a Secondness—but is a state. Feeling has no consciousness of itself—that would involve a concept, Thirdness. The experience of Firstness, according to Peirce, is

> an instance of that kind of consciousness which involves no analysis, comparison or any other process whatsoever, nor consists in whole or in part of any act by which one stretch of consciousness is distinguished from another, which has its own positive quality which consists in nothing else, and which is of itself all that it is, however it may have been brought about. [1.306]

Firstness is very difficult to talk about, "is so tender that you cannot touch it without spoiling it" (1.358), because immediate feelings can only be contemplated in memory, which "is an articulated complex and worked-over product which differs infinitely and immeasurably from feeling" (1.379). Even though Firstness is insusceptible to thought (that is, we experience it as a feeling), Peirce does not conclude that we are somehow out of touch with the immediate, leading lives of delusion, peril, and deception in prison houses and over bottomless abysses. He sums it up thus:

> [W]hatever is in the mind in any mode of consciousness there is necessarily an immediate consciousness and consequently a feeling.... [T]he feeling [is] completely veiled from introspection, for the very reason that it is our immediate consciousness.... [A]ll that is immediately present to a man is what is in his mind in the present instant. His whole life is in the present. But when he asks what is the content of the present instant, his question always comes too late. The present is gone by, and what remains of it is greatly metamorphosized. [1.310]

Just as immediate feeling is the consciousness of Firstness, a sense of polarity or reaction is the consciousness of Secondness. Again, Peirce's examples clarify his general, often vague, statements:

> Besides Feelings, we have Sensations of reaction; as when a person blindfold[ed] suddenly runs against a post, when we make a muscular effort, or when any feeling gives way to a new feeling.... Whenever we have two feelings and pay attention to a relation between them of whatever kind, there is the sensation of which I am speaking. [6.19]
>
> . . . .
>
> While I am seated calmly in the dark, the lights are suddenly turned on, and at that instant I am conscious, not of a process of change, but yet of something more than can be contained in an instant. I have a sense ... of there being two sides to that instant. A consciousness of polarity would be a tolerably good phrase to describe what occurs. [1.380]

The consciousness of a process of change negated in the above quotation is the consciousness of Thirdness:

> This is a kind of consciousness which cannot be immediate, because it covers a time, and that not merely because it continues through every instant of that time, but because it cannot be contracted into an instant. It differs from immediate consciousness, as a melody does from one prolonged note. Neither can the consciousness of the two sides of an instant, of a sudden occurrence, in its individual reality, possibly embrace the consciousness of a process. This is the consciousness that binds life together. It is the consciousness of synthesis. [1.381]

In consciousness, feelings are Firstness; reaction-sensations or disturbances of feelings are Secondness; and general conceptions are Thirdness.

Having briefly defined Firstness, Secondness, and Thirdness, we are ready to relate these categories to Peirce's three trichotomies.

THE TRICHOTOMIES

According to Peirce's analysis of his own definition, a sign is one of three kinds (Qualisign, Sinsign, or Legisign); it relates to its object in one of three ways (as Icon, Index, or Symbol); and it has an interpretant that *represents* the sign as a sign of possibility, fact, or reason (that is, as Rheme, Dicent Sign, or Argument). The strange words in this paragraph constitute the last of the new terms needed to prepare for a discussion of art, criticism, and theory within a Peircean theory of signs.

The accompanying chart shows the relation of the categories and the trichotomies. Subsequent discussion will reveal that every embodied sign (that is, every triadic sign) involves formal Firstness, Secondness, and Thirdness, but not necessarily all the material categories of Firstness, Secondness, and Thirdness. I present it in full awareness of the commonly held notion that Peirce is not clear about whether his categories are ontological or phenomenological. I do not find Peirce to be inconsistent on this matter: he shows that signs signify because of their qualities *and* their relations. The material aspects are predominant in a Qualisign; the relational or formal aspects, in a Symbol or Argument. A Saussurean linguist who focuses only on the formal character of linguistic signs obviously sees only the relational-differential character of the sign.

Phenomenological or formal categories		Ontological or material categories		
		Firstness	Secondness	Thirdness
Firstness	A sign is:	a "mere quality" QUALISIGN	an "actual existent" SINSIGN	a "general law" LEGISIGN
Secondness	A sign *relates* to its object in having:	"some character in itself" ICON	"some existential relation to that object" INDEX	"some relation to the interpretant" SYMBOL
Thirdness	A sign's interpretant *represents* it (sign) as a sign of:	"possibility" RHEME	"fact" DICENT SIGN	"reason" ARGUMENT

Peirce holds that the material aspects of Firstness, Secondness, and Thirdness are empirically observable. The material aspects of Firstness, as I have already mentioned, Peirce calls quality, the immediate nonconceptual given of sense experience. The material aspect of Secondness Peirce calls "Thisness," the immediate, nonconceptual experience of the dynamic interaction of two things. Existence is dyadic. Depending on one's definition of "ontological," the concept of a material aspect of ontological Thirdness may cause some confusion. What Peirce has in mind is the experience of thought or rationality. Ontological Thirdness has much less the character of the immediate given than have the other two categories, but according to Peirce,

> the third category—the category of thought, representation, triadic relation, mediation, genuine thirdness, thirdness as such—is an essential ingredient of reality, yet does not by itself constitute reality, since this category ... can have no concrete being without action, as a separate object on which to work its government, just as action cannot exist without the immediate being of feeling on which to act. [5.436]

Thus, the material aspect of Thirdness is analogous to that of *langue* as described by Saussure.

Formally, or phenomenologically, Peirce holds that "signs may be divided as to their own material nature, as to their relation to their objects, and as to their relations to their interpretants."[5] Peirce holds that all thought is reducible to some combination of these three and that this triadic relation is irreducible. He was later to increase the number of formal categories, but he never revised the concept of a triadic relation of sign-object-interpretant.

"A *Qualisign*," according to Peirce, "is a quality which is a sign. It cannot actually act as a sign [be represented] until it is embodied [in a triad of sign-object-interpretant]; but the embodiment has nothing to do with its character as a sign" (2.244). In the beginning was a sign, and that sign was with a quality, and that sign was a quality. In Peirce's cosmogonic philosophy and sign theory, all reality and signs have evolved from qualities. The only way a Qualisign can be represented is thus:

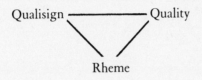

Otherwise, the Qualisign becomes part of the object of another triadic relation, such as:

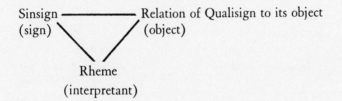

Now it should be clear why pure Firstness and Secondness, Qualisigns and Sinsigns, respectively, are difficult to talk about. They cannot be linguistic signs. No sign can be a word (written or spoken) until it has become a triad of Thirdnesses. A Firstness must undergo three transformations or generations before it can be represented by a word. By now I think my following use of abbreviations for sign, object, and interpretant and for Firstness, Secondness, and Thirdness will not be too confusing:

S   "positive qualitative possibility"

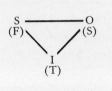

a sign in the mind (feelings) of Firstness, a Qualisign

a sign in the mind of a sign in the mind, a Sinsign

a sign or symbol (possibly a word) in the mind for a sign in the mind of a sign in the mind, a Legisign

If one understands the above, he or she already understands Sinsigns and Legisigns. A Sinsign is a sign that is a fact. Or, in Peirce's words, it "is an actual existent thing or event which is a sign" (2.245). The syllable *sin*, Peirce tells us, is taken as meaning "being only once." It can be only once in the sense that it is always and only the second transformation; that is, it is "an actual existent thing or event which is a sign," its object is an embodied Qualisign, and its interpretant is the only Thirdness in the sign. It may be visualized thus:

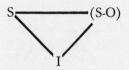

Every Legisign is a sign that represents the relation of a sign in the mind to a sign in the mind. Just as the objects of Sinsigns are embodied Qualisigns, the objects of Legisigns are embodied Sinsigns. And just as Qualisign is a sign that is a quality and Sinsign "is an actual existent thing or event which is a sign," so is Legisign "a law that is a Sign." "This law is usually established by men. Every conventional sign is a Legisign. . . . It is not a single object, but a general type which, it has been agreed, shall be significant" (2.246). Since it is a general law and not a quality or actual existent object, "every legisign signifies through an instance of its application, which may be termed a *Replica* of it. Thus, the word 'the' will usually occur from fifteen to twenty-five times on a page. It is in all these occurrences one and the same word, the same Legisign. Each single instance of it is a Replica" (2.246). But the Replica would not be significant "if it were not for the law which renders it so" (2.246).

A quick reference to Peirce's definitions of Icon, Index, and Symbol reveals that only a Legisign can be a Symbol, that is, "a sign which would lose the character which renders it a sign if there were no interpretant" (2.304). A Sinsign may be Index or Icon. As Index, it is "a sign which would, at once, lose the character which makes it a sign if its object were removed, but would not lose that character if there were no interpretant" (2.304). As Icon, it is "a sign which would possess the character which renders it significant, even though its object had no existence" (2.304). Of course, a Qualisign can be only an Icon. When Peirce is describing his ten classes of signs (which I will discuss at the beginning of the next chapter), he frequently uses the adjectival form for the signs in his second trichotomy (e.g., Iconic) because Icon, Index, and Symbol are concepts (signs) that describe the relation of a sign to its object.

Interestingly, Peirce's definition of a sign is consistent with the linguistics of Wittgenstein. In contrast, Saussure's definition of the sign as dyadic, together with his failure to bring the activity of mind into his treatment of signs, has been an obstacle to the application of Wittgenstein's linguistic turn in literary criticism and poetics. The implication one gets from Saussure's linguistics is that language is something arbitrarily added to preexisting objects. This concept has led frequently to a misunderstanding of the linguistic turn as merely a reversal of this process—beginning with language rather than with being. It is not as though we experience language and the world as independent entities; we come to the world through language or, more precisely, through language games— "modes of activity which involve intentional actions, in accord with rules and norms, directed toward purposeful ends."[6] This is the same argument Peirce makes for his definition of a sign as a triadic relation of sign-object-interpretant. Wittgenstein and Peirce both insist that we have no choice but to unite linguistic signs, objects, and mental activity (interpretants) in one notion and treat them as dependent rather than independent entities. The implications this has for intention and meaning will be treated later. Having reviewed Peirce's definitions of a sign, his three categories, and his trichotomies, we are now ready to see what implications his theory of signs has for literary aesthetics, criticism, and theory.

[6] Richard Fleming, review of William Barrett, *The Illusion of Technique* (New York: Doubleday, 1978), in *Auslegung: A Journal of Philosophy* 6 (November 1978): 68.

FIVE

Art: Meaning as a Sign
of Possibility

Hurrah for positive science! long live exact
   demonstration!
. . . .
Gentlemen, to you the first honors always!
Your facts are useful, and yet they are not my
   dwelling,
I but enter by them to the area of my dwelling.

—Walt Whitman, "Song of Myself"

This chapter is concerned with what Peirce's theory of signs
shows us about the character of a literary text and aesthetic
experience. Given the irreducible triadic sign, which includes
the interpretant (a sign stands to *somebody* for *something* in
some respect), we cannot be "objective" and "subjective" alter-
nately; the text and our experience of it are given together.
Everything is always *for us*. But we can show what kind of a
sign a literary text is according to Peirce's theory of signs and
how near we can come to the thing-in-itself, the literary text
in this case.

In order to do this we need to review Peirce's classification
of signs. The following diagram of his ten classes of signs is
less complex than the one Peirce provides, but it is easier to
understand and adequate for the present purpose. Note that

each line represents one of Peirce's classes of signs and that the numbers indicate the order in which Peirce presents them.

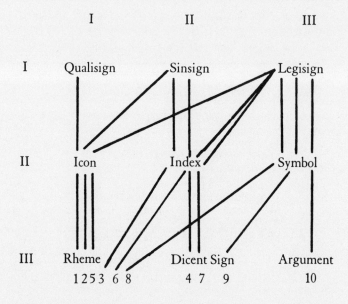

        I   II   III

I   Qualisign   Sinsign   Legisign

II   Icon   Index   Symbol

III   Rheme   Dicent Sign   Argument
        1 2 5 3 6 8   4 7   9   10

Based upon the fact that Qualisigns and Sinsigns are Firstness and Secondness, respectively, and upon the hypothetical process of sign generation noted above, classes 1 through 4 cannot be linguistic signs; that is, they cannot be words or sounds emitted from a person to signify. The interpretant of a Qualisign can be no more than a feeling. A Sinsign is already a combination of signs in that it is always an object of experience (actual existent) that points to another object of experience. Of interest here is the fact that at a more basic level of experience than linguistic signs, we already have *syntax*, a combination that signifies by the nature of the relationship.

The last six classes involve Legisigns, but classes 5, 6, and 7 are not necessarily linguistic. 😊 I take to be an Iconic Legisign, but I cannot imagine a word that is an an Iconic Legi-

sign, except maybe one like "G__d." Even when they are linguistic signs (e.g., the demonstrative pronoun "that" is a
Rhematic Indexical Legisign), they are general laws, habits, or
conventions that (as Icons and Indices) picture and point,
draw attention to objects other than themselves.

Classes 8, 9, and 10 are all Symbols; they draw attention to
themselves, to their formal properties, as much as to their referential significance. These are the classes of signs of primary
interest to our discussion because, as we shall see, literary art,
criticism, and theory are class-8, -9, and -10 signs respectively.
The following brief comparison of the interpretants and the
modes of meaning of these classes of signs may also be read as
a comparison of literary art, criticism, and theory.

In early formulations Peirce had called his interpretants
Terms, Propositions, Arguments. He later changed the first
two of these because at best they were appropriate only to
classes 8, 9, and 10; that is, appropriate to signs that are Symbolic Legisigns. Moreover, the class-8 sign, the Rhematic
Symbol, can be a much more complex sign than "Term" implies because it can embody a virtually unlimited number of
objects. It can be a word, sentence, or book (2.292). The term
"Proposition," however, is not misleading so long as we are
talking about a class-9 sign, and I will sometimes use it instead
of Dicent Symbol in the following discussions simply because
it is more familiar. The differences between class-8, -9, and
-10 signs lie principally in the different ways in which they
represent their objects. The interpretant of a class-8 sign, a
Rheme, "is a Sign ... of qualitative possibility, that is, is
understood as representing such and such a kind of possible
Object.... [It is] a sign which is understood to represent its
object in its characters merely" (2.250, 2.252). The interpretant
of a class-9 sign, a Dicent Sign, "is a sign which is understood
to represent its object in respect to actual existence" (2.252).
And the interpretant of a class-10 sign, an Argument, "is a
Sign which is understood to represent its Object in its char-

acter as a Sign" (2.252). The peculiarity of each sign, Peirce says,

> lies in its mode of meaning; and to say this is to say that its peculiarity lies in its relation to its interpretant. The proposition professes to be really affected by the actual existent or real law to which it refers. The argument makes the same pretension, but that is not the principal pretension of the argument. The rheme makes no such pretension. [2.252]

It is an interesting observation that, generally speaking, "-ology" disciplines, such as theology, biology, anthropology, deal with arguments or theories, interpretants that are assured or verified by their "Form," their character as signs. The "-ic" disciplines, such as logic, ethics, physics, and linguistics, deal with existent relations, interpretants assured by "Experience." Saussure's conception of *Semiology* as a "science of signs" and Peirce's conception of *Semiotic* as synonymous with logic may account for the suffixes they employed. Most important to our present concern is the fact that all the arts, literary art included, are signs of qualitative possibility, interpretants assured by "Instinct" or conviction.

Peirce does not write extensively about art as sign, but he makes clear in various writings that art always partakes of the mode of being of Firstness as well as of Secondness or Thirdness. Literary art, being inseparable from language, of course partakes of Thirdness (is a Symbol), but it creates an interpretant that has the mode of being of Firstness (is a Rheme). For example, Peirce says that if we allow his categories to form our conceptions of history and life, "we remark three classes of men"—men who create art, practical men who carry on the business of the world, and men possessed with a passion to learn. The first class "consists of those for whom the chief thing is the qualities of feelings. These men create art" (1.43). The artist contemplates actual existence as an aesthetic spectacle, cultivates the feelings of immediate consciousness, celebrates the possible and the role of the possible. That which is actual interests him only to the extent that his artistic imagination can invest it with poetical possibilities. For these persons "nature is a picture" (1.43).

The second class is made up of persons who "respect nothing but power, and respect power only so far as it [is] exercised" (1.43). These persons seek methods to control themselves and their environments, usually in order to facilitate fulfillment of their own desires. Finally "the third class consists of men to whom nothing seems great but reason" (1.43). Those familiar with Peirce will recognize that these are in Peirce's view the "natural scientific men," who inquire "into truth for truth's sake, without any sort of axe to grind, nor for the sake of the delight of contemplating it, but from an impulse to penetrate into the reason of things" (1.44).

We can surmise that if Peirce had put literary artists, critics, and theorists into these classes, he would have put the literary artists in the first class; the critics, who carry on the practical business of reading and interpreting texts, in the second; and theorists among the true scientists of the third class. However, if the literary theorist is a philosopher "with a system which he thinks embodies all that is best worth knowing," or has any motive other than "truth for truth's sake" as do "chemists who occupy themselves exclusively with the study of dye-stuffs," he is not, according to Peirce, a true scientist (1.44–45).

The intent of the present chapter is to clarify the definition of literary art as "a sign of qualitative possibility" that represents "possible objects" in their "characters merely." Peirce says, "A Sign may *itself* have a 'possible' Mode of Being."[1] That is, we may conceive of signs as "possible," not connected with events, actual existents, or acts of reason, but as signs of

[1] 23 December 1908, *Charles S. Peirce's Letters to Lady Welby*, ed. Irwin C. Lieb (New Haven, Conn.: Whitlocks, 1953), p. 31.

the immediate, unanalyzable, inexplicable, unintellectual consciousness that "runs in a continuous stream through our lives" (5.289). The material qualities or characters that belong to a sign apart from its representative function, and the capability of a sign to be connected with another sign, Peirce says, can be described only as feelings and possibilities until they are predicated or objectified by subsequent signs (5.286–287). The representamen of a class-8 sign is represented by its interpretant as a sign of possible objects in their character merely—hence as a sign of the feeling, the quality of immediate consciousness, of what is in the mind in the present instant (1.310). Literary art, according to Peirce, is such a representamen of possibility experienced as Rhematic Symbol. Even though it may represent many propositions and arguments, as for example a work of fiction frequently does, these are seen in context as signs of possibility. Art, then, presents us with *signs of* immediate consciousness, that is, feelings, qualities, Rhemes. Aesthetic experience is our experience of a class-8 sign—that is, "feeling, the consciousness which can be included with an instant of time, passive consciousness of quality, without recognition or analysis" (1.377).

As shown in the preceding chapter, the elements of phenomena in Peirce's ontological categories of Firstness, Secondness, and Thirdness, are quality, fact, and thought, respectively. Like all linguistic signs, the signs of literary art are triads involving signs of ontological Thirdness (are Symbolic Legisigns). But art is unique in that its interpretant is a sign of ontological Firstness (is a Rheme). In art, Thirdness represents (symbolizes) the qualities of ontological Firstness. Peirce tries numerous times to help us understand what it means to be a sign of quality. He says, for example:

[T]he idea of a quality is the idea of a phenomenon ... considered as a monad, without reference to its parts or components and without reference to anything else. We must not consider whether it exists, or is only imaginary, because existence depends on its subject having a place in the general system of the universe. An element separated from everything else and in no world but itself, may be said, when we come to reflect upon its isolation, to be merely potential. [1.424]

Peirce's definition of a Rheme is consistent with this idea of quality. Even though Peirce makes it clear that a class-8 sign, a Rhematic Symbol, may be a word or an entire text, his definitions of a Rheme are meant to be applicable to all classes of signs involving Rhemes, and he typically uses simple examples to make his points. However, a simple Rhematic Symbol (a word) has the same mode of being as a complex one (a novel). "A rheme," he says, "is any sign that is not true or false, like almost any single word except 'yes' or 'no,' which are peculiar to modern language." Also, he says a Rheme can be thought of as "simply a class-name or proper-name."[2] Wittgenstein's comments on naming seem to express the same idea:

> Naming is ... not a move in the language-game—any more than putting a piece in its place on the board is a move in chess. We may say: *nothing* has so far been done, when a thing has been named. It has not even *got* a name except in the language-game. This is what Frege meant too, when he said that a word only has meaning as part of a sentence.[3]

A Rheme, Peirce says, "perhaps, will afford some information; but it is not interpreted as doing so" (2.250). The Rheme, that is, the aesthetic experience of a literary text, has the same relation to ontological Secondness or Thirdness that a word

---

[2] 12 October 1904, ibid., p. 13.
[3] Ludwig Wittgenstein, *Philosophical Investigations*, trans. G.E.M. Anscombe (New York: Macmillan, 1958), p. 24.

has to a sentence, that a name or chess piece has to its use in a game. By itself, it merely stands as a sign of possibility.

Martin Heidegger's treatment of the nature of art, in *Poetry, Language, Thought*, helps us to see what it means to think of art as a sign of ontological Firstness. He says, "The art work opens up in its own way the Being of beings. This opening up, i.e., this deconcealing, i.e., the truth of beings, happens in the work."[4] Heidegger has several useful analogies to explain what happens to "being" in human consciousness. For example, he says that in human cognition the world is perceived as earth and sky, divinities and mortals. That which is art gathers and unites the fourfold; it "stays the fourfold into a happening of the simple onehood of world."[5] This happening, he says,

> cannot be explained by anything else nor can it be fathomed through anything else. . . . As soon as human cognition here calls for an explanation, it fails to transcend the world's nature, and falls short of it. The human will to explain just does not reach to the simpleness of the simple onefold of worlding. The united four are already strangled in their essential nature when we think of them only as separate realities, which are to be grounded in and explained by one another.[6]

This is the same point Peirce makes when he says,

> The immediate present, could we seize it, would have no character but its Firstness. Not that I mean to say that immediate consciousness (a pure fiction, by the way [because by its very character the immediate is not susceptible to mediation, i.e., consciousness]), would be First-

---

[4] Heidegger, *Poetry, Language, Thought*, trans. Albert Hofstadter (New York: Harper & Row, 1971), p. 39.

[5] Ibid., p. 181.

[6] Ibid., pp. 179–180.

ness, but that the *quality* of what we are immediately conscious of, which is no fiction, is Firstness. [1.343, bracketed material added]

It is impossible to talk about Firstness without losing it. When we try to bring the content of the present instant to consciousness, the sensation is past, has become the predicate of a subsequent sign, and "what remains is greatly metamorphosized" (1.310).

Since a poem (any work of literature) is experienced as a Rhematic Symbol, it is a distortion to equate it with a Proposition or Argument—perhaps an enlightening distortion, but a distortion nevertheless. The disdain of literary critics for moralistic and subjective interpretations of art is well known, but is a little like the pot calling the kettle black. The nature of art and the dynamic nature of signs as defined by Peirce's theory of signs reveal the limitations and pitfalls of the critical process. Anytime one says anything about the Rheme produced by the reading of a text, he is unconsciously allowing the interpretant (Rheme) to become a new representamen, which determines a new interpretant (another Rheme, a Proposition, or an Argument). In other words, he turns a sign of imaginative possibility into a new sign of imaginative possibility, a Proposition, or an Argument.

Strictly speaking, the critic has only a memory of experiencing a poem, and his comments are inadvertently about his memory of experiencing the poem, that is, about his memory of the poem's interpretant. The plight of the critic is that the literary work, like any other sign, is dynamic and unceasingly generating new interpretants. It is for him always already in a peculiar relation to an interpretant. There is no single right reading of a literary work, not only because a literary work is a complex sign but also because, as is true of any sign, it always generates interpretants that in turn become signs and so on to infinity. The literary text as sign is not something fixed and permanent that will stand still to be looked at. It is always alive, unceasingly generating interpretants that are always interpreted by subsequent thoughts. The implications this has for hermeneutical theorists, such as E. D. Hirsch, who wish to distinguish between understanding and interpretation will be treated in subsequent chapters.

However, we should at least pause here to point out that the traditional critical notion of autonomy must be revised in light of the above definition of literary art as a class-8 sign, a Symbolic Rheme. The idea of artistic autonomy is often defended by appealing to Kant's aesthetic theory. Peirce was greatly influenced by Kant and, except for his abjuring of Kant's "proposition that a thing-in-itself can, however indirectly, be conceived" (5.452), Peirce's treatment of art as a sign of possibility is consistent with Kant's treatment of aesthetic experience in his *Critique of Judgment*.[7]

Kant, like Peirce and Wittgenstein, distinguishes between the expressive and the cognitive; aesthetic judgment and propositions about actual existents; purposiveness and consciousness of purpose; that for which there are no rules for synthesis and that which is determined by such rules; that which is incapable of proof and that which demands proof; that which makes no ontological claim about the aesthetic object and that which is concerned with actual existence; a consciousness whose determining ground is feeling and a consciousness whose determining ground is objective rules; an experience of a sign whose autonomy is not so much self-sufficiency as possibilities of synthesis in cognitive and practical experiences and an experience of a sign as dependent on the rules of logic. However, the very term "autonomy" belongs to the objectivist tradition of thinking and suggests characteristics for a text that are totally inconsistent with a theory of

[7] See *The Critique of Judgment*, trans. James Creed Meredith (Oxford: Clarendon Press, 1952), pp. 61–80.

triadic signs. A literary text is certainly not autonomous in the sense that it exists separately from any interpretant, any sign in the mind—that is an idealistic, mystical notion. Even Hirsch, who argues that a text's meaning is determinate, is in agreement with us on this point.[8] For us, there are no texts-in-themselves; there are no aesthetic objects apart from Rhematic interpretants; there are no literary objects except as denoted in signs subsequent to those in which representamens of a text are embodied. Every object that we try to isolate is for us already embodied in a set of relationships that gives it meaning.

The word "text," as the foregoing paragraph implies, also belongs to the tradition of objectivist thinking and causes confusion. A literary work of art is not the same as the print on the page. According to Peirce's theory of signs, there is not a static, fixed, literary object "out there" apart from any reading of it. The paper and the graphics are not the literary work. The marks on the page are not the full portrayal of the sign system, of the language if you will, in use by the author or the reader. A sign is always a triadic relation of representamen, object, and interpretant, which in turn creates another sign in which the interpretant becomes the representamen and so on. In print, we do not have the whole signifying process modeled or illustrated. Printed language is, as it were, only the representamen of the total sign. Since the object and the interpretant are not on the page graphically, we think they are "outside" the text. If a literary work were merely "text," inkmarks on the page, that would be true; for a reader, however, the representamen, object, and interpretant are present in every sign experienced. These signs-in-the-mind come to us in connection with some ground or language game, and consequently with their meaning or possible meaning (and inten-

[8] E. D. Hirsch, Jr., *Validity in Interpretation* (New Haven, Conn.: Yale University Press, 1967), p. 23.

tion, as we will see in the next chapter). The relationship of the printed page to the literary work is more like the relationship of the power line to the electricity that travels along and around it than it is like the relationship of parts to a whole.

The image of electricity flowing along power lines reminds us that even though we have considered a text as *a* sign in order to clarify the mode of being of a discussion of that work, we also need to come to terms with the fact that a poem or novel is not experienced as one sign. A succession of signs makes up a literary work just as a series of instants makes up consciousness. It is the continuity that is the medium or mediation of consciousness. Thus, a work of art symbolizes the "feeling" of experiencing the "possible" successive awarenesses and interpretations of signs. As readers, we "hypothetically" see how it is with other sign users; but, of course, we do not get out of our minds into theirs. As we follow their fictional adventure in signs, our own thoughts keep spinning off in subsequent signs that interpret our own experience. The notion that we can follow the author's train of thought, sequence of signs, without ever intruding with a thought of our own, the notion that we can have a pure experience of the text without adding a subsequent thought of our own, is a notion we should abjure from the bottom of our hearts for the same reasons Peirce abjured Kant's thing-in-itself. It goes against everything we have learned about the triadic, dynamic nature of signs. The signs of literary art, whether words, sentences, or entire books, are *for us*; we experience them as signs of quality, and we experience many of them in subsequent signs in which they are interpreted.

Although we attribute to literature the character of being a sign of possibility, we are confronted with hundreds or thousands of signs of every linguistic type. Peirce gives us an example illustrating how many sign relations are involved in a very simple sentence:

[T]he statement, "Cain killed Abel" cannot be fully understood by a person who has no further acquaintance with Cain and Abel than that which the proposition it-self gives.... But further, the statement cannot be understood by a person who has no collateral acquain-tance with killing.... Of course, an Icon would be nec-essary to explain what was the relation of Cain to Abel, in so far as this relation was *imaginable* or imageable. To give the necessary acquaintance with any single thing an index would be required. To convey the idea of causing death in general, according to the operation of a general law, a general sign would be requisite; that is a *Symbol*. For symbols are founded either upon habits, which are, of course general, or upon conventions of agreement, which are equally general.⁹

Whether the mode of meaning of the sign "Cain killed Abel" is that of a Rheme or Proposition is determined by the ground with which the sign relates to its interpretant. Since a Sym-bolic Rheme makes no pretension to be really affected by ac-tual existents or real laws to which it refers, the propositions embodied in it are understood in their "possible" mode of being without contradicting the fact that a proposition "pro-fesses to be really affected by the actual existent or real law to which it refers" (2.252). Thus, in fiction we do not understand the meanings of signs that have the form of propositions to be factual, about actual existents. A proposition, Peirce says,

may be contemplated as a sign capable of being asserted or denied. This sign itself retains its full meaning whether it is actually asserted or not. The peculiarity of it, therefore, lies in its mode of meaning; and to say this is to say that its peculiarity lies in its relation to its inter-pretant. [2.252]

⁹ 14 December 1908, *Letters to Lady Welby*, p. 24.

To be sure, the signs of a novel are capable of having meaning within a multitudinous number of grounds or language games. Many of them are capable of being understood in the mode of meaning of Dicent Signs and Arguments as well as that of Rhemes. But to the degree that the novel is a class-8 sign, to the degree that it is art, to the degree that it is fictional, its signs have the mode of meaning of a Rheme and are signs of the quality of immediate consciousness. The mode of meaning of all literature *as art* is that of a Rhematic Symbol. That is why we say a novel as a sign with its totality of objects is a class-8 sign, *not* a class-9 or -10 sign. It does not symbolize life as it actually is or was; it does not symbolize the laws to which events will conform in the future; rather, it symbolizes the qualities and feelings of the immediate, which "runs in a continuous stream through our lives" but is insusceptible to consciousness because cognition or representation always involves the relation, the binding together of previous cognitions. Thus, according to the view of art presented here, the question to be confronted concerning so-called autonomy is whether it is possible in our experience to distinguish between the aesthetic experience of a literary text and an interpretation of it. This question will be addressed in the next chapter. But it should already be clear that Gerald Graff can speak of "truth statements" as literature if he wants, but not of literature as truth statements.[10]

Peirce, though no artist or art critic, saw the significance of art to be its quality of Firstness, not its conventions of Thirdness. I intend to show later that it is their focus on Thirdness, on the symbolic, formal, conventional character of language, that makes it impossible for many of the current literary theorists to distinguish literature from other uses of language.

[10] Graff, see *Literature against Itself: Literary Ideas in Modern Society* (Chicago: University of Chicago Press, 1979).

Wittgenstein, who had a lifelong interest in aesthetics and used parables and fables in his own writing, was well aware that poetry expresses the sense of life that cannot be described in factual terms. "What expresses *itself* in language," he said, "*we* cannot express by means of language." "What *can* be shown," he added, "*cannot* be said."[11] Particularly in his early work, Wittgenstein stressed that there is a fundamental difference between the use of language in mythology and in art and the use of language in rational, discursive thought. In the former, language is consciously used *indirectly* to *show* imaginative possibility; in the latter, it is used *descriptively* to *say*, to state fact. The accompanying chart shows how easily the positions of Peirce and Wittgenstein may be integrated.

RHEMATIC SYMBOL————————Interpretant——DICENT SYMBOL

INDIRECT COMMUNICATION —Sign———— DESCRIPTIVE LANGUAGE
Language used to "show"   Language used to "say"
  poetry   myth   propositions
  drama   satire   science models
  fiction   fable
        irony

POSSIBLE VALUES————————Object———— ACTUAL FACTS
assurance: conviction   assurance: operational test

Language (formal and ontological Thirdness) can be used to symbolize ontological Firstness (to show) and Secondness (to say). It goes without saying that language can symbolize itself; that is, it can be a symbol that represents a symbol (i.e., Argument or Third-Thirdness) partaking of, but not limited by, other modes. But to the degree that we experience a literary work as a class-8 sign, as a representation of ontological First-

[11] Wittgenstein, *Tractatus Logico-Philosophicus*, trans. D. F. Pears and B. F. McGuinness (London: Routledge & Kegan Paul, 1961), p. 51.

ness, as a representation of the "sense" of life, as signs of immediate consciousness in their characters merely, we "feel" it rather than "think about" it, "see" it rather than "describe" it.

With the view of art presented in this chapter, we can once again conceive of art in a way that has been out of fashion in recent years. Peirce gives us a theoretical basis for such descriptions of art as the following:

> All arts create symbols for a level of reality which cannot be reached in any other way. A picture and a poem reveal elements of reality which cannot be approached scientifically. In the creative work of art we encounter reality in a dimension which is closed for us without such works. . . . A great play gives us not only a new vision of the human scene, but it opens up hidden depths of our own being. Thus we are able to receive what the play reveals to us in reality. There are within us dimensions of which we cannot become aware except through symbols, as melodies and rhythms in music.[12]

Allen Janik and Stephen Toulmin, in their book *Wittgenstein's Vienna*, interpret the *Tractatus* as presenting a view of language that, they say,

> assigns a central importance in human life to art, on the ground that art alone can express the meaning of life. Only art can express moral truth and only the artist can teach the things that matter most in life. Art is a mission. To be concerned merely with form, like the aesthetics of the 1890s [and the 1980s, we might add], is to pervert art.[13]

[12] Paul Tillich, *Dynamics of Faith* (New York: Harper & Brothers, 1957), pp. 42–43.
[13] *Wittgenstein's Vienna* (New York: Simon & Schuster, 1973), p. 197.

And Peirce himself wrote, "So the poet in our days—and the true poet is the true prophet—personifies everything, not rhetorically but in his own feelings. He tells us that he feels an affinity for nature, and loves the stone or the drop of water."[14]

Such views of the artist and his work are rarely put forward by structuralists because their conception of signs provides no theoretical basis for them. Peirce's pragmaticism makes room for such views without making him sound like Pollyanna. In his theory of signs there is no contradiction between these descriptions of art and the assertion by many modern intellectuals, from Sigmund Freud to Peter Handke, that humans are alienated from themselves and unable to escape the prison house of language. Without denying that we cannot escape from language, from Thirdness, Peirce shows us that Thirdness (linguistic, symbolic signs) can symbolically represent Firstness. According to his theory of signs, literary art is language (Rhematic Symbol) used to show, picture, symbolize the quality of immediate consciousness that can never be immediate to consciousness.

Our desire for origin and presence is not nearly so metaphysical as Derrida would make it seem. The "being" of art is to symbolize the quality (the feeling) of the immediate, which "runs in a continuous stream through our lives." If we deny or totally ignore being and assume that form (linguistic structures, differance) is all, we will find nothing unique about art. This has been the experience of the deconstructionists. Actually, absolute idealism and realism are both far more metaphysical than anything in Peirce's pragmaticism. Peirce refuses to think of signs as purely formal or to think of the real apart from signs. His claim is that our experience is not broader than signs, but that it is broader than the signs in our

[14] *Charles S. Peirce: Selected Writings (Values in a Universe of Chance)*, ed. Philip P. Weiner (New York: Dover Publications, 1958), p. 13.

conscious thought. Art does not just give us the unreal, the pure play of form in our imaginations; it gives us symbols that make us aware of more of our experience in the world of signs, more of what is for us the real.

While human experience is broader than linguistic signs, human rationality is not. Hence the cleavage between art and criticism which we will discuss in the next chapter.

SIX

Criticism:
Meaning as a Sign of Fact

> When language-games change, then there is a change in concepts, and with the concepts the meanings of words change.
>
> —Ludwig Wittgenstein, *On Certainty*

Peirce's theory of signs provides the means by which we can get beyond the tradition of objectivist thinking about language and art that has both undercut the validity of interpretation and divorced literature from meaning and human experience. This chapter shows how a triadic definition of a sign influences our understanding of literary criticism and other interpretive acts.

The separation of language and meaning, objects and contemplating subjects into autonomous parts in objectivist thinking has had the effect of separating literature from lived experience, from reading and criticism. Whether it is the poem that is autonomous, as I. A. Richards claims, or all of language that is autonomous, as deconstructionists assert, the effect is the same: the impossibility of reading *the text* or arriving at *its* meaning. Both the text and its meaning are placed outside the world we experience. We know only language which, the deconstructionists say, always displaces presence and defers meaning. While language makes us believe that there are texts and a world that have meaning, it always holds them beyond our reach like a carrot on a stick. Finally, according to their theory, we have had the courage to face up to the real truth that the carrot is an illusion, that human experience is characterized by blindness, alienation, and deferred meaning.

When we begin with Peirce's definition of a sign, the theory of "gaps" must give way to a theory of "grounds"; the theory that separates text and meaning must give way to a theory in which sign-object-interpretant are inseparable. Language, human action, and world are inseparably united in the triadic sign. A sign is always a combination of a representamen, object, and interpretant in a particular use; that is, a sign is a dynamic, triadic relation of representamen, object, and interpretant within a certain ground.

In the preceding chapter, we showed that the grounds of aesthetic experience, of Rhemes, are consistent with the mode of meaning of class-8 signs and are feelings, not cognitions, and that there are, therefore, no rules or objective standards for determining or validating such interpretants. Criticism, on the other hand, is a class-9 sign according to Peirce's sign theory and claims both to represent its object (a literary text) "in respect to actual existence" and to "really be affected by the actual existent or real law to which it refers" (2.252). Here the grounds become objective rules, and a sign may have multiple grounds just as does a picture within a picture in a house in a novel. For the sake of clarity I will speak of "ground" in an inclusive sense.

Peirce's general conclusion about interpretation, which is applicable to science and logic as well as to literary criticism, is that the only exactitude or certainty Dicent Signs have is relative to a particular ground. After evaluating the claims of certainty based on revelation, the axioms of geometry, the principles of logic, historical proof, and direct experience, Peirce concludes:

[W]e cannot in any way reach perfect certitude nor exactitude. We never can be absolutely sure of anything,
nor can we with any probability ascertain the exact value
of any measure or general ratio. . . .

. . . .

But it would be quite misunderstanding the doctrine of
fallibilism to suppose that it means that twice two is
probably not exactly four. As I have already remarked,
it is not my purpose to doubt that people can usually
count with accuracy. Nor does fallibilism say that men
cannot attain a sure knowledge of the creations of their
own minds. It neither affirms nor denies that. It only
says that people cannot attain absolute certainty concerning questions of fact. [1.147, 1.149]

Peirce acknowledges that there is nothing new in this doctrine and that many of the greatest minds of all time have held
it (1.148). The challenges to reason of Kant and Kierkegaard
come to mind immediately. But Peirce is careful to distinguish
between a statement of fact and a statement about a system of
our own creation (1.149). Any "if . . . then" statement is of the
latter sort, and all science, logic, and literary criticism must
acknowledge that they can make no certain statement of fact
and that there is an "if" implicit or explicit in all their asser-
tions.[1]

It is this "if" that gives *subjectivity*, *relativity*, and *certainty*
to interpretations. At the basis of all rationality is a nonrational act, a volitional choice. The description, explanation, or
interpretation of anything is grounded in prior choices and
commitments. The grounds can be rationally investigated, as
can the grounds for the investigation and so on to infinity.
Wittgenstein says that, at some point, questioning must come
to an end in order for us to act. At that point, we accept a

[1] E. D. Hirsch, Jr., makes a similar point in *Validity in Interpretation* (New
Haven, Conn.: Yale University Press, 1967), p. 91.

certain ground (language game or use of language) and begin from there as rational human beings. Kierkegaard argues that "the beginning of logical and rational systems must lie in a 'leap'—the 'leap' being the introduction of some willful resolve or act which is not itself open to the rational questioning and reflection that keep rational inquiry from having a rational basis."[2] Gadamer concludes, "[T]here is undoubtedly no understanding that is free of all prejudices, however much the will of our knowledge must be directed towards escaping their thrall. It has emerged throughout our investigations that the certainty that is imparted by the use of scientific methods does not suffice to guarantee truth."[3] Hirsch defines his aim as "validation" of interpretation rather than "verification," acknowledging that "the fact that certainty is always unattainable is a limitation which interpretation shares with many other disciplines."[4]

In order to act, in order for a sign to have any meaning, in order to "make" sense of the text, we choose a ground or, as Hirsch says, make a guess.[5] All rational systems, all thought, all experience of Thirdness are grounded by and in the free but necessary choice of sign users—authors, readers, thinkers. Any interpretation of a text, therefore, must be seen within the broader perspective of human volition, just as every act of reason itself proves to be an act of will and depends on a free but necessary choice of a human being for its use and validity. A sign cannot be separated from its object/interpretant and the ground determining the significance of the triadic relation.

---

[2] Richard Fleming, "Remarks on Reason" (University of Kansas diss., 1982), p. 31.

[3] Hans-Georg Gadamer, *Truth and Method* (New York: Seabury Press, 1975), p. 446.

[4] Hirsch, *Validity in Interpretation*, pp. 164, 170–171.

[5] Ibid., pp. 170, 203, 207.

Peirce's "ground," as defined here (and in Chapter 4), and Wittgenstein's "language games" are similar if not exactly the same. Language games as rule-governed activities provide the frame of reference for all use of linguistic signs. "When language games change, then there is a change in concepts, and with the concepts the meaning of words change."[6] The meaning of a poem or any other sign always involves a ground (Peirce sometimes substitutes the term "idea") or language game that it produces or modifies. These games are public, shared, part of one's culture and controlled by rules; the choice of a language game that determines the meaning of signs is, however, private and not controlled by rules.

A similar comparison can be made between Peirce's "ground" and what Hirsch calls "genre," what Heidegger calls "world," and what Gadamer calls "horizon" (i.e., "situatedness," "historicity," "linguisticality"). I do not imply that these terms are interchangeable, but that they are the "ground" of understanding and interpretation for each of these thinkers. Genre, world, or horizon, like ground or language game, is presupposed in every act of knowing. The experience of a literary work, like the experience of any sign, is not outside these contexts, but through them. "Language games," Gadamer says, "are where we, as learners—and when do we cease to be that?—rise to the understanding of the world."[7] "The act of understanding," Hirsch says, "is at first a genial (or a mistaken) guess, and there are no methods for making guesses, no rules for generating insights."[8]

Subjectivity and relativism, then, are inevitable. We make

[6] Ludwig Wittgenstein, *On Certainty*, ed. G.E.M. Anscombe and G. H. von Wright, trans. Denis Paul and G.E.M. Anscombe (New York: Harper & Row, 1969), p. 10e.

[7] Gadamer, *Truth and Method*, p. 446.

[8] Hirsch, *Validity in Interpretation*, p. 203; he makes a similar statement on p. 170.

choices. Whether those choices are conscious or unconscious is not of primary concern here. Most of what has been said by philosophers, social scientists, and literary theorists about *a priori* propositions, foreknowledge, foremeaning, codes, cultural conventions, language games, grounds, etc. could be drawn on to make this point more forcefully.

But this subjectivity is very limited and circumscribed, virtually lost as it is exercised. Relativism does not mean that there is no truth, but that truth is not outside and above time, place, and history; it does not mean there are no standards for judgment, but that there are many. Given a particular ground, a qualifying and relativizing "if," the force of reason and logic and the certainty of interpretation cannot be meaningfully questioned. But if the goal is complete and final answers, definitive rational explanations (which the present book in no way pretends to offer), that project is doomed because the answers and explanations are relative to the choice (ground, assumptions) on which they are based. Another person may reject one choice (and therefore the explanation or interpretation) and offer another choice every bit as forceful as the one he rejects.

Our inability to achieve a complete, final, or rational understanding of anything not only shows the impossibility of final interpretations (Peirce places them as always in the future, as I will show in the next chapter) but shows the limitations of all rational systems and inquiries. I think that one of the reasons Saussure and Derrida are as successful with their systems as they are is that they are incomplete in a radical way—they leave out everything existential, even the role of sign users, and retain only abstract form.

In Peirce's theory of signs, all rational investigations involve centrally the role of the human subject. There are no signs in thought apart from the sign-object-interpretant relation. That accounts, to a great extent, for the differing conclusions of Peirce and Derrida about intention, context, and meaning. In

his writing on speech-act theory[9] Derrida's logic goes something like this: since meaning is context-bound, intentions do
not determine meaning; since context is boundless, meaning
is never full or final, never within grasp. By objectifying
meaning, setting it apart from use, from signs, from statements, Derrida will always find it to be "exterior" to language. Peirce and the others I have quoted in the preceding
pages incorporate context and human lived experience (meaning) into the sign system. Peirce would, of course, agree with
Derrida that "final meanings" are out of the question, but
would insist that there is no escaping the human being or the
free and necessary choice involved in all sign usage. In order
to signify, a sign, or representamen, must stand for something
(its object) to somebody (its interpretant) in reference to the
ground, language game, or concept that is the nonrational
choice of the human subject (2.228). The choice is free, in that
there are no rules governing it, and the possibilities are numerous; it is necessary because no sign in the mind is possible
without a ground. There is no sign that acts as a sign apart
from a contemplating subject, and there is no gap between
sign and meaning, because every sign embodies the relationship of its representamen to its object and interpretant according to some ground or language game. Sign, object, and
meaning come to us together or not at all. Their relationship
is primary. This theory is vastly different from those which
assume that language is an arbitrary, strictly formal system
independent of human action and actual existents; the implications for criticism are numerous. The traditional critical
concepts of autonomy, intention, understanding, and interpretation must be radically revised to conform with the theory
of language based on a triadic sign.

I have already shown in the preceding chapter that auton-

---

[9] See particularly Derrida's "Signature Event Context," *Margins of Philosophy*, trans. Alan Bass (Chicago: University of Chicago Press, 1982), pp.
307–330.

omy can mean nothing more than is implied in the fact that a literary text is a class-8 sign, a Symbolic Rheme. Since there are no objects apart from the triadic sign, the question to be confronted concerning so-called autonomy is whether it is possible in our experience of a literary text to distinguish between aesthetic experience and interpretation.

UNDERSTANDING AND INTERPRETATION

Not only is interpretation influenced by the free but necessary and determining choice of ground, but the dynamic nature of signs is even more problematic. The dynamic nature of signs has been described earlier in this book, but a fuller treatment of it here may help clarify what is involved in the attempt to distinguish between aesthetic experience and interpretation, understanding and interpretation. Peirce does not use the terms "understanding" and "interpretation" in presenting his theory of signs, but he does talk extensively about percepts, perceptual facts, and criticism (which for him is synonymous with rational thought, reasoning). Percepts, Peirce says, constitute experience proper and are not within our control. A perceptual fact, the intellect's judgment of the evidence of the senses, is an imperfect record of percepts, at best. Because the perceptual judgment represents itself as an index or true symbol of a percept, "we find ourselves impotent to refuse our assent to it in the presence of the percept" (7.628). Of course, we can look again and assure ourselves that we did perceive what we thought we perceived, but ultimately it is our percepts upon which we rely. All criticism or reasoning depends on perceptual facts. But criticism cannot begin until a judgment is formed. It begins with premises that represent percepts or generalizations of such percepts (2.140–145, 2.773). Thus, perceptual facts and criticism are pretty much synonymous with "understanding" and "interpretation." Since these terms are fundamental to the aesthetic and interpretation the-

ory of such writers as Martin Heidegger, Hans-Georg Gadamer, and E. D. Hirsch, Jr., I feel compelled to adapt Peirce's
theory to these terms as much as possible in order to appreciate and evaluate the differing positions of these writers.

First, let us consider Peirce's perception of how the dynamic character of signs influences interpretation. Cognition,
Peirce says, is a process. "Whenever we think, we have present to the consciousness some feeling, image, conception, or
other representation, which serves as a sign ... *to* some
thought which interprets it" (5.283). Every thought-sign is interpreted by a subsequent thought. From this principle Peirce
concludes:

> [Since] there is no intuition or cognition not determined
> by previous cognitions, it follows that the striking in of
> a new experience is never an instantaneous affair, but is
> an *event* occupying time, and coming to pass by a contin-
> uous process. . . . [E]very thought-sign is translated or in-
> terpreted in a subsequent one, unless it be that all
> thought comes to an abrupt and final end in death.
> [5.284]

Not only is a sign interpreted in a subsequent thought, it
also stands *for* some object by denoting the previous thought.
The only way a sign can stand for a real outward thing is by
referring to it through the denoting of previous thought. Since
we are conscious only of previous signs, immediate consciousness is not possible. Thought, to the degree that it is immediately present, can be no more than an "absolutely simple and
unanalyzable" feeling, "a mere sensation without parts,"
"simply an ultimate, inexplicable fact" (5.289). Therefore, we
never know the thought-in-itself; for, before we can make the
reflection "this is present to me," the sensation "is past, and,
. . . once past, we can never bring back the quality of the feeling as it was *in and for itself*, or know what it was like *in itself*"
(5.289). The thought present in the mind at a certain instant

is meaningful only by virtue of its relation to subsequent interpretant-thoughts that give us information about their objects reflectively. Meaning, then, lies "not in what is actually thought [immediately present], but in what this thought may be connected with in representation by subsequent thoughts; so that the meaning of a thought is altogether something virtual" (5.289). Meaning is the dynamic relation of signs; life is a train of thought.

Peirce says that every sign creates an interpretant that relates the sign to its object within a certain ground. This interpretant, or sign-in-the-mind, is the "meaning" or "understanding" of that particular sign. A text of a literary work (note the distinction) mediates new events that we will understand, just as we do all events, simultaneously with our experience of them, instantaneously, without necessarily being conscious of the ground or foreknowledge that makes our understanding possible. Since the more novels we read and discuss the more we understand in other novels, we speculate that foreknowledge increases, that we do in fact learn from experience, that previous interpretants are incorporated into new triadic signs. But what we understand is the event—not the print, not the author, not an aesthetic object, not the world out of which the text came. We are in the event, the happening; for us, experience and meaning are interdependent and inseparable. The meaning (i.e., understanding) of *Nicholas Nickleby* is that signs symbolizing subjects and people and events of the novel occur in our experience.

"Understanding" cannot be separated from what we refer to as "experience of the literary work" or "reading." There is no work apart from "understanding." "Understanding" is our grasp of signs *in use*, of the language game we are *in*. "Understanding" is co-original with our use of signs, with our lived experience, with our language games. It is the interpretant of the sign. It is *not* an object or entity, but our mode of experiencing signs. "Understanding" is contextual, determined not by the character of transcendental objects or the whims of transcendental subjects, but by genre (Hirsch), presuppositions (Kant), horizons (Gadamer), world (Heidegger), ground (Peirce), language games (Wittgenstein).

But the sign's object is "interpreted" by the triadic sign-object-interpretant relationship. Thus, every sign involves both understanding (of a sign or representamen) and interpretation (of the sign's object). If, for example, the interpretant of *Nicholas Nickleby* (a Rheme) becomes a new sign with a new ground, the interpretant of the new sign "understands" the new sign but "interprets" the preceding one. Signs understood in use become interpreted objects in subsequent signs. The only evidence we have of our "understanding" is the subsequent thought in which it is "interpreted." Our "thinking about" *Nicholas Nickleby*, whether we call that interpretation, application, making judgments, or criticism, is likewise an event in which experience and meaning, ground and interpretation are inseparable. In other words, "understanding" is use of signs; "interpretation" is objectifying or thinking about an earlier sign.

Thus, Peirce's definition of the sign as a dynamic, triadic relation gives us a frame of reference to appreciate and evaluate the differing positions of Gadamer and Hirsch in regard to understanding and interpretation. Gadamer, unlike Heidegger and Hirsch, says the distinction between understanding and interpretation is an abstraction because, in praxis, "interpretation is not an occasional additional act subsequent to understanding, but rather understanding is always an interpretation."[10] Within the context of Gadamer's concern with the "event" of understanding, with the "general task of establishing the ontological background of the hermeneutical experience of the world,"[11] his conclusions are consistent with

[10] Gadamer, *Truth and Method*, p. 274.
[11] Ibid., p. 441.

Peirce's theory of signs. He seems to recognize that, in Peircean terms, a sign's relation to its interpretant (understanding) and a sign's representation of its object "in some respect" (interpretation) come together in every sign and are inseparable relationships. Even though at points Gadamer seems to acknowledge that there is an ontological difference between understanding and interpretation (for example, he says that "the appearance of the beautiful and *the mode of being* of understanding have the character of an event," and that "interpretation is the *explicit form* of understanding"),[12] his persistent refrain is that all understanding is an event involving interpretation and, hence, we cannot distinguish them in experience. Gadamer's philosophical hermeneutic is an effort to account for what *is*, what happens in, the experience of understanding, of encountering, of seeing. In the face of what is, the question of validity, the establishing of normative principles for judging correctness, is somewhat beside the point. This is particularly true of aesthetic experience, which is not translatable into propositions and is, along with ethics and metaphysics, that about which Wittgenstein says we must be silent.

Even though Gadamer is ready to move beyond "substance metaphysics" and "the metamorphosis of the concept of substance into concepts of subjectivity and scientific objectivity," even though he is ready to leave behind the task of "justifying, in terms of the theory of science, the claim to truth of art and the artistic,"[13] many of his readers, Hirsch among them, are not ready for such moves. They, still viewing Gadamer's work from within the tradition of objectivist thinking that he critiqued, find his treatment of understanding, interpretation, and application fuzzy and inadequate.

Even though Hirsch and Kant work within the objectivist

---

[12] Ibid., pp. 441, 274; italics added.
[13] Ibid., p. 441.

tradition, their distinctions between understanding and interpretation and between aesthetic judgments and cognitive judgments, respectively, are in some ways comparable to Peirce's theory. Since Hirsch's entire program for validating interpretation rests on *his* distinctions between understanding, interpretation, judgment, significance, and criticism, a brief review of his definitions is in order. "Understanding," Hirsch says, "is a perception or construction of the author's verbal meaning, nothing more, nothing less." "Interpretation" is "an *explanation* of meaning." In its "pure form," interpretation is "paraphrase or translation," but it is "almost always mixed with criticism." In making the distinction between a text's "meaning" and its "significance," Hirsch says that "one understands meaning; one judges significance." "Significance" is "any perceived relationship between construed verbal meaning and something else." He proposes to use the term "interpretation" for "commentary that is primarily about meaning," and to use the term "criticism" for "commentary that is primarily about significance."[14]

> [I]nterpretation and criticism are both present in all textual commentary and . . . the two functions can be distinguished only by deciding which goal is preeminent, but I think it important to remind ourselves of these different goals, if only to make clear that significance is distinct from criticism in precisely the same way that meaning is distinct from interpretation. Criticism is not identical with significance, but rather refers to it, talks about it, describes it.[15]

Even though Hirsch says that "understanding, interpretation, judgment, and criticism are distinct functions with distinct requirements and aims" and takes Gadamer to task for trying

[14] Hirsch, *Validity in Interpretation*, pp. 136–143 et passim.
[15] Ibid., pp. 143–144.

"to topple one of the firmest distinctions in the history of hermeneutic theory, that between the *subtilitas intelligendi* and the *subtilitas explicandi*—the art of understanding a text and the art of making it understood by others," he admits that in the act of construing the meaning of the text such distinctions cannot be made.[16] This is Gadamer's very point. But Gadamer would also probably object to Hirsch's claim that "at the level of the discipline these two 'moments' or 'episodes' [i.e., understanding and explaining] can be separated in a way that they cannot be in the course of construing a text."[17] However, Peirce's sign theory would support Hirsch's claim. Insofar as we are concerned, for heuristic purposes, with a particular sign's interpretant as an "object of knowledge," as Hirsch refers to both meaning and significance, Hirsch's distinction between understanding and interpretation is useful and is consistent with the concept of the dynamic, triadic sign.

Although Hirsch's claim that "understanding," or the text's "verbal meaning," is determinate, changeless, reproducible, and is the author's willed intention, not to mention Hirsch's effort to use "author's intention" as a test for validity of interpretation, is not totally consistent with Peircean theory, his concept of "understanding" as "silent" and "prior" to interpretation is (as I will show later) in some ways consistent with Peirce's theory. "Understanding," Hirsch says, is a "silent" grasp of the meaning in the text's terms; "interpretation" is what gets written down—in the interpreter's terms, of course.[18] According to Peirce's theory of signs, as pointed out earlier in this chapter, not only "understanding" of literary works, but any interpretant (sign-in-the-mind; i.e, *all* "understanding") is silent. What is spoken or written down is not a triadic sign, but merely its representamen. Therefore, neither understanding nor interpretation gets "written down."

[16] Ibid., pp. 133, 253.
[17] Ibid., p. 206.
[18] Ibid., pp. 135–136.

Rather, signs (representamens, words) of the text create interpretants that we call "understanding" of the text; but, for us, understanding and text are one and the same thing. Interpreters write and speak using representamens that are other than the representamens of the text but whose "objects" are the signs of the text *as understood in the interpreter's previous interpretants*. Insofar as the signs of the text are represented by the representamens of the interpreter, they are represented with respect to the grounds of the interpreter's representamens.

The theoretical basis on which Hirsch distinguishes understanding from interpretation is not the above, but the objectivist "gap" theory, which holds that one cannot *say* anything about a work without supplementing it. Hirsch says, for example:

> Since our interpretations are always other than the language by which they are construed, a space of uncertainty exists between the vehicle (our language of cognition) and the meanings (or objects) interpreted from it. This gap, which cannot be overcome, is a space in which different interpretations can be played out. Hence, there is always an element of uncertainty in every possible sphere of interpretation. This gap of uncertainty is the defining feature of interpretation—the gap between . . . the vehicle and the meaning, between the sign and the signified.[19]

Surely it is clear by now (if not, it should become so in the next few pages) that the theoretical "gap" between language and meaning which Hirsch says cannot be overcome does not exist in a theory of interpretation based on a triadic sign. Language and meaning are not separable. However, the free and

---

[19] E. D. Hirsch, Jr., "The Politics of Theories of Interpretation," *Critical Inquiry* 9 (September 1982): 236.

necessary choice of grounds involved in all sign use, coupled with the fact that signs are interpreted in subsequent signs in Peirce's theory, has an effect similar to the one Hirsch ascribes to the "gap" in the above quotation. There is a sense in which interpretations are "always other than the language by which they are construed" because of the dynamic nature of signs. Therefore, there is a near parallel in Peirce's theory to Hirsch's theory that understanding ("a perception or construction of the author's verbal meaning") is "silent" and "prior to" interpretation (an explanation of that meaning) and significance ("any perceived relationship between construed verbal meaning and something else").[20] In Peircean terms, Hirsch's position might be stated as follows: anytime one *says* anything about the Rheme produced by the sign, he is unconsciously allowing the interpretant of the class-8 sign (Rheme) to become a new sign that determines a new interpretant. Strictly speaking, the speaker has only a memory of experiencing a Rheme (which is the same as saying a poem, since it is the only poem there is for him). Everything one *says* relates that memory to something else that determines its "significance" (Hirsch's term).

In other words, interpretation and criticism are not signs whose interpretants are Rhemes (understanding, verbal meaning) created by the text as sign, but are signs chosen by the interpreter to relate the text's verbal meaning to a particular ground, that is, "to categories and conceptions that are not native to the original."[21] Signs of the latter sort are propositions that are true or false; that is, they are signs of fact that pretend to be really affected by their object (the text's verbal meaning, in this case) and, as such, are subject to the tests of evidence and probability with which propositions are vali-

[20] Hirsch, *Validity in Interpretation*, pp. 135–143.
[21] Ibid., p. 136.

dated. Hence, there is a sense in which Hirsch is consistent with Peirce in saying that interpretation is not "a perception or construction of" the meaning of the signs of the literary text proper, but is an explanation of the construed meaning. Likewise, criticism construes not the text's verbal meaning (understanding, Rheme), but its "significance"—that is, the perceived relationships between the text's verbal meaning and something else—and the "significance" of a text is constantly changing.

Thus, the criticism of Hirsch for asserting the primacy of silent understanding over interpretive explanation[22] needs to be qualified. Certainly Peirce would not accept Hirsch's claim that the text's verbal meaning (understanding) is the same for every reader, determined by the author's intention and not at all influenced by the perceiving subject. And while he would agree with Gadamer that all understanding involves interpretation, there is a sense in which "understanding" of *a particular sign* is prior to "interpreting" *that* sign. For example, Peirce says: "A Dicisign [another term for Dicent Sign] necessarily involves, as part of it, a Rheme, to describe the fact which it is interpreted as indicating" (2.252). In this sense, interpretation rests on the earlier operations of understanding. Every sign incorporates into its object earlier signs, that is, previous understandings and interpretations. Even though there is never a time when any sign or meaning is experienced prior to interpretation or reader involvement (since every sign is embodied in a triadic relation including sign-object-interpretant), the understanding and interpretation, the use and the objectifying of *a particular sign* or representamen do not occur in the same triadic sign. Yet, one might ask, is everything said about a work true or false, subject to the test of

[22] See, for example, David Couzens Hoy, *The Critical Circle: Literature, History, and Philosophical Hermeneutics* (Berkeley: University of California Press, 1978), pp. 13–24.

correctness? Must every judgment follow rules of logic or reason? These are questions addressed by Kant in his *Critique of Judgment*. In fact, if we compare Kant's treatment of "aesthetic objects" to Peirce's treatment of Symbolic Rhemes and percepts, we find much similarity.

Kant's concept of an aesthetic object as having "free beauty" (beauty that "presupposes no concept of what the object should be," nor any end or purpose in the representation)[23] is very similar to Peirce's concept of literary art as a "sign of possibility." Kant's distinction between "expressive" judgments and "cognitive" judgments—the first of which have as their ground the "feeling of the Subject"; and the latter, "objective rules"[24]—is very like Peirce's distinction between Rheme and Dicent Sign. Kant claims that aesthetic judgments make no ontological claim about the aesthetic object and are neither true nor false.[25] Hence, aesthetic judgments are not constructions of the author's meaning (interpretation) or judgments of the relation of the text's verbal meaning to something else according to the rules of logic or ethics (criticism), as Hirsch argues, but are judgments expressive of "feeling" and are not bound by rules of "cognition." In Peircean terms, the aesthetic judgments are class-8 signs, just as are literary works, with which we attempt to express more for ourselves than for anyone else (2.252) the Rhematic interpretant, which is more "feeling" than "cognitive" thinking. But in saying something is beautiful, expressing feelings, we are not somehow "closer" to the work than we are in subsequent signs that have the mode of meaning of Dicent Signs. Aesthetic judgments are subsequent signs determined by previous cognitions in which the sensation of the beautiful,

[23] *The Critique of Judgment*, trans. James Creed Meredith (Oxford: Clarendon Press, 1952), pp. 61–63, 72–74.
[24] Ibid., p. 75.
[25] Ibid., p. 55.

worked over and greatly metamorphosized in memory, is predicated.

Although we may be content with making only aesthetic judgments about painting or music, we are rarely if ever satisfied to leave a literary work without making cognitive judgments about it. Apparently, we need to incorporate the experience of the text into our life world, to make something of it or, as Hirsch says, to relate it to something else. Gadamer maintains that "understanding always involves the application of the meaning understood."[26] This is what we generally think of as interpretation, and what Peirce calls class-9 signs. Such a conception of interpretation, or of signs, requires that we allow our Rhematic interpretant to create a new sign that determines an interpretant that is a Dicent Sign or Proposition, terms I use interchangeably. Or, in more traditional terms, we put the work (actually our memory of the work) into contexts, like putting a word into sentences. We use the language games we know, our horizons of expectation, and make sense of it according to the rules of rational thought, of human cognition. We say something about it; we treat it as predicate, as object.

INTENTION

For most of us, the questions of intention (and intentionality) and validity do not arise until cognitive judgments are made about the work. We want to know whether an interpretation is the "real" meaning, the "true" meaning, an "accurate" meaning, a "valid" meaning, the "author's intended" meaning. Hirsch says that *correct* "understanding" is determined by the author's intention and that a *valid* "interpretation" is one that, even though it explains the meaning in terms famil-

---

[26] Gadamer, *Truth and Method*, p. 297.

iar with the interpreter and audience and not necessarily those of the text, grasps the words of the text in the sense originally intended by the author.[27]

Hirsch's conception of author's intention cannot be supported using Peirce's theory of signs. First of all, the notion that there is a particular meaning (which we might better call a particular "experience," since it is silent) that the writer intended to provide is a strange one even if we accept the fact that it is impossible to verify what the intention is. Does a short-story writer, a painter, a ballerina intend to create in the interpreter a particular experience with each sentence, brush stroke, movement? Or does an artist, rather, intend a story, a painting, a dance? Are there right and wrong experiences? From Hirsch's insistence that the author's intended meaning is public, shared, and reproducible, rather than anything private, I gather that he would agree that an author cannot decide the rules of a language game or the meaning of words within a certain ground. The author's intention, then, cannot differ from the rules of the game or ground he chooses. Wittgenstein treats this point extensively. He says, for example: "[W]hat kind of super-strong connexion exists between the act of intending and the thing intended?—Where is the connexion effected between the sense of the expression 'Let's play a game of chess' and all the rules of the game?—Well, in the list of rules of the game, in the teaching of it, in the day-to-day practice of playing."[28]

A game has its being, its rules, not in the consciousness or actions of the players.[29] The intentions and actions of the players are not separable from the games they are in. If a player enters a game, it is probably safe to assume that his intention is to play the game. What are the purposeful ends of the

---

[27] Hirsch, *Validity in Interpretation*, p. 136.
[28] Ludwig Wittgenstein, *Philosophical Investigations*, trans. G.E.M. Anscombe (New York: Macmillan, 1958), p. 80.
[29] Gadamer, *Truth and Method*, pp. 95–96.

game? It is our objectivist thinking that causes us to try to separate a player from the game, the author from the work.
Would we think to ask a basketball player his intentions in
playing a particular game of basketball? If we did ask, the
only answers that would make sense to us would merely re-
peat the rules and purposes of the game. If he said his intentions were to break the left leg of an opponent, we would
know he was talking about another game than the one we
know as basketball and would ask him what game he intended to play. If he said that the game of basketball is for
him an opportunity to play a game of revenge, the confusion
would be cleared up. At game time, we would understand his
actions according to the rules of the game he chose to play.
Intention, language game, and meaning are not separable
concepts; they are not outside our experience but are the very
means of it. Neither are they separable from literary works;
there simply are no signs-in-the-mind without them. The author's intention, then, cannot differ from the rules of the language games or grounds he chooses. Neither can a reader's
perception of intention differ from the language games or
grounds he (the reader) chooses. And what remains beyond
absolute verification is whether or not these grounds or intentions are the same for the author and the reader.

Peirce would agree with Gadamer that there is no text independent of the human mind, and of those expectations and
possibilities of understanding that characterize the interpreter's life world (Gadamer calls these historicity and linguisticality, and they are synonymous with language games and
grounds). Consequently, the author's intention that Hirsch
wishes to use to test the validity of interpretations can be nothing other than Hirsch's own intention, that is, the intention of
the language game he chooses. Intention is certainly involved
in all signs and in all interpretation. But what we call "author's intention" is merely a shorthand way of identifying the

ground that determines the interpretant of the signs we experience. *Every* linguistic sign is perceived as intended. Attributing the intention to the author is a political move that both allows us to claim authority and objectivity for our understanding of the text and shifts the responsibility for our interpretations off our shoulders onto the author or text. It is not much different from shifting the responsibility for our actions to God's will, fate, or potty training. It is not John Steinbeck or *The Grapes of Wrath* but the fundamentalist Christians wishing to ban the book who are preoccupied with immorality. It is their choice that makes obscene Rose of Sharon's breast-feeding a starving man after her baby has died. Another choice on their part would have made the scene a portrayal of the kind of charity we find in Christ's sacrificial death, as the name Rose of Sharon implies.

Gadamer nor Wimsatt, Beardsley, or anyone else that I know of denies that we should try to understand the author's intention, that is, the grounds, language games, horizons within which the author works. They rightly deny the possibility of ever establishing that intention definitively as well as the necessity of doing so. Intention, meaning, understanding all describe *our* experience as sign users. They are *for us*. In a section of *Truth and Method* dealing with the temporal distance between the creation of the text and the interpretations of it, Gadamer makes the following statements:

> The real meaning of a text, as it speaks to the interpreter, does not depend on the contingencies of the author and whom he originally wrote for. It certainly is not identical with them, for it is always partly determined also by the historical situation of the interpreter and hence by the totality of the objective course of history.
>
> . . . .
>
> Not occasionally only, but always, the meaning of a text goes beyond its author. That is why understanding is not

merely a reproductive, but always a productive attitude
as well.

. . . .

[T]he discovery of the true meaning of a text or work of
art is never finished; it is in fact an infinite process.[30]

Gadamer's conclusions seem like radical subjectivism to
Hirsch, who thinks of a text as an autonomous, independent
object, with a determinate, unchanging meaning, and who
wants to arrive at the correct knowledge about it. So long as
we think of art as an object, we, like Hirsch, will wonder
about its relation to other experiences we objectify, such as
reality, inner experience, and the author's life. But Hirsch's
concerns and the grounds for his attack on Gadamer lose their
force once we step outside the tradition of objectivist thinking.
Gadamer's conclusions are totally consistent with what is implied about meaning in Peirce's theory of signs. Both Gadamer and Peirce are concerned about validity and truth, but
they look at these within the context of the sign system or
language within which the *process* of understanding and interpretation occurs.

VALIDITY

Having established the subjectivity involved in interpretation,
and having reconstituted and recentered humans, so to speak,
let us now turn to the questions of certainty and validity. It
should be clear by now that meaning for Peirce is *in* the triadic
signs, not outside them. Meaning is not something in addition
to language. Signs and meaning come together in our experience. However, even though meaning is *for us*, it is never private, or occurring only once. It is inseparable from custom,
use, institutions. All linguistic signs are Legisigns; that is, they
are signs that are social conventions, public "laws," generals.

[30] Ibid., pp. 263, 264, 265.

According to Peirce, we experience these in an irreducible triadic relation with objects and interpretants in reference to grounds or language games. We cannot separate language, human activities, and meaning. Language and our world come to us inseparably united in the triadic relation of signs, objects, and interpretants within the context of public, shared, rule-governed human activities. If we want to know what can be validly said about a text, we must take Wittgenstein's advice and "look and see" what happens in *use*, in practice, and learn from that. One cannot judge an interpretation against an object, but against the actions and practice in which it is grounded, against the rules of the language games in use. The rules (laws, habits) that govern the *use* of signs are finally what make meaning possible and are the only objective test of validity or correctness. This is not, however, a simple solution to the question of validity.

It may be useful to distinguish between "certainty" and "validity." We have already conceded that certainty as absolute knowledge about the state of things is not within human grasp. But we also use "certainty" to describe what Peirce calls personal conviction, belief, and habit. In his essay "The Fixation of Belief" Peirce distinguishes among doubt, belief, and validity. The feeling of believing, he says, indicates that there has been established "some habit which will determine our actions [and which] ... puts us into a condition that we shall behave in a certain way when the occasion arises" (5.371–372). All that Peirce maintains about "belief" is that we seek beliefs that will "truly guide our actions so as to satisfy our desires" and "that we shall *think* to be true" (5.375). But he is quick to point out that reasoning is valid when it leads to an awareness of fact and truth. Facts, Peirce says, are "hard things that do not consist in my thinking so and so" (2.173), and truth consists in "the existence of a real fact corresponding to the true proposition" (2.652).

Where, then, does that leave us in our search for reality and truth in literary criticism? Peirce's concepts of reality and truth are consistent with his theory of triadic, dynamic signs and are therefore future-oriented. Peirce refuses to treat the "real" as incognizable or independent of representative relation. It makes no sense to Peirce to define the real as "incognizable" because that is to claim knowledge about what is defined as unknowable. Rather, he encourages us "to regard the appearances of sense as only signs of realities. Only, the realities which they represent would . . . be . . . intellectual conceptions which are the last products of the mental action which is set in motion by sensation." The "last products" referred to here are the final and definite opinions "to which the mind of man is, on the whole and in the long run, tending."[31] "The real," Peirce says,

> is that which, sooner or later, information and reasoning would finally result in, and which is therefore independent of the vagaries of me and you. Thus, the very origin of the conception of reality shows that this conception essentially involves the notion of a COMMUNITY, without definite limits, and capable of a definite increase of knowledge. [5.311]

The same goes for truth: "there is . . . to every question a true answer, a final conclusion, to which the opinion of every man is constantly gravitating."[32] Individuals may not live to reach the truth, and general agreement may be postponed indefinitely, but "that cannot affect what the character of that opinion shall be when it is reached."[33]

Our situation is that we never experience objects except through previous signs and that we are not even conscious of

[31] "Critical Review of Berkeley's Idealism," *Charles S. Peirce: Selected Writings (Values in a Universe of Chance)*, ed. Philip P. Weiner (New York: Dover Publications, 1958), pp. 83, 82.
[32] Ibid., p. 81.
[33] Ibid., p. 82.

particular signs except as they are denoted in subsequent signs. Therefore, "everything which is present to us is a phenomenal manifestation of ourselves." However, Peirce says, "this does not prevent its being a phenomenon of something without us, just as a rainbow is at once a manifestation both of the sun and the rain" (5.283). Since Peirce sees reality and thought as interdependent, rather than incompatible, he can say, "There is nothing ... to prevent our knowing outward things as they really are, and it is most likely that we do thus know them in numberless cases, although we can never be absolutely certain of doing so in any special case" (5.311). We might add, parenthetically, that this is equally true of our knowledge of author's intentions.

Because Peirce's concepts of truth and reality are future-oriented, they cannot be used as a measure of validity in the special cases, the particular judgments and opinions of individuals that we are concerned with when the question of validity arises. About all that can be said is that, both in practice and in the final opinion toward which our individual opinions are tending, validity depends on agreement. A "valid" interpretation is one consistent with agreed-upon principles or rules. Or, put another way, the validity of an argument consists in the fact that it pursues a method (e.g., inductive reasoning) "which, if duly persisted in, must, in the very nature of things, lead to a result indefinitely approximating to the truth in the long run" (2.781).

According to Peirce's theory of signs, we at least have some justification for the sense of certainty we have about our existential experience. Unlike the dyadic sign in which the world is lost in the crack, gap, abyss of nothingness, or whatever, the triadic sign gives us faith that we do indeed come to the world through signs, and the objects of experience do have meaning for us that is understandable to others whether or not they agree with the correctness of our views. Because of the general nature of signs, because all use of language, all perception of meaning is rule-controlled, nearly any meaning experienced by anyone could be shown to be in accord with rules, with belief, with (as we will see in the next chapter) theory. If one person takes a particular statue to be a pagan idol, another takes it to be a naked women, and still another takes it to be the goddess Ceres, each has "grounds" for what he or she sees and no one will deny that they all see the same object. Or, as Gadamer says, no one denies that Jews and Christians share the same Old Testament; their interpretants are different because their grounds are different. The validity of a statement about a poem, statue, or scripture, is determined by the frame of reference or the language game.

However, the appeal to commonly agreed upon rules as a standard for validity has its limits of practicality and usefulness. We rarely agree on the "right" rules for testing validity. Critics and schools of criticism have tried, and will no doubt continue to try, to privilege a few rules for interpretation of literary works and to claim that valid interpretation must proceed according to their rules. But there will always be public debates and disagreements about valid interpretations for a number of reasons, all having to do with the nature of signs.

First, readers' subjective choices of grounds or language games that will determine their ideas of order about the work are not, and cannot be, controlled by rules. Consequently there will be differing interpretations, each of which will claim that the rules or grounds determining it are the "right" ones to be used. To appeal to reason, to seek validation, is to appeal to understanding based on uninvestigated presuppositions. The triadic sign within a ground provides reason with the aspect of reality with which it will work. Reason stands within language games in the same way signs do. This was Wittgenstein's point in the *Tractatus*, when he pointed out that it is hard to be illogical because language is logical. Hirsch's appeal to evidence and probability is nothing more than an appeal to our understanding of whether or not rules are being followed. The question "Is that reasonable?" is basically "Is that consistent with the rules of any game you know?" We answer such questions, "Well, if this is the case (game, context), then . . . yes, but if . . . no." In practice, the question of validity is, "Is this interpretation consistent with the rules we have agreed on?"

Second, we learn the use of signs without consciously learning the rules that make possible the use of signs. We learn the customs of making reports, giving orders, obeying rules, reading texts as literature or as science, as truth or fiction. Structuralists and semioticians have had a heyday discovering what must be the rules governing nearly every human activity, from arranging food on a plate to arranging the political values within a culture. Although many language games have been identified and described, most have been learned practically and without any explicit rules. Since we learn practices and uses, there is no way of establishing a causal relation between the rules and the meaning experienced. Meaning and use are the same; we always already have them. The citing of rules is justification of meaning, after the fact so to speak. Most criticism is just such a description of language game rules as justification of interpretation. Northrop Frye's theory of modes, Wayne Booth's rhetoric of fiction, Roland Barthes' codes come to mind immediately in this respect. Even if we are persuaded by their cogent arguments and agree with them about the rules governing fiction, the difficulty is still not over. The possible applications of a rule are virtually unlimited, and whether or not a particular application of a rule is consistent with the rules is also a matter of (dis)agreement. Consider the numerous different ways of applying the rule that author's intention should determine interpretation. Hirsch is hardly ready to go along with the way Steven Knapp and Walter Benn Michaels apply the rule.[34]

[34] See Steven Knapp and Walter Benn Michaels, "Against Theory," *Crit-*

Third, signs are dynamic relations, not static objects or marks on a page. Therefore meaning, too, is dynamic and takes place in the motion of signs, comes to pass in the continuity of consciousness. Peirce's theory of signs shows us that our individual interpretant "is nothing but another repesentation to which the torch of truth is handed along; and *as a representation*, it has its interpretant again. Lo, another infinite series" (1.339).

Symbols grow, and possible relations between symbols increase. The character of symbols is to stand in *some* relation to other symbols. The possibilities of such relations are limitless. To try to find the rules that control the creation of new symbols and language games is like trying to fathom a black hole in space. Despite Peirce's penchant for classification,[35] there is no reason to believe that he would have disagreed with Wittgenstein's demonstration of the unlikelihood of ever finding a few common rules that will be applicable to all language games.[36]

Practically speaking, then, the validity of interpretation has no basis other than agreement among persons about the application of agreed-upon rules and is always open to question. The effort to justify interpretation is integral to literary criticism, but is never complete. These facts are consistent with the dynamic nature of signs and are in no way a threat to meaning. It does not follow from them that there is no mean-

---

ical Inquiry 8 (Summer 1982): 723–742, and the response by E. D. Hirsch, Jr., "Against Theory?" *Critical Inquiry* 9 (June 1983): 743–747.

[35] In his later years, Peirce further elaborated his theory of signs. He distinguished two objects of a sign, each of which had ontological Firstness, Secondness, and Thirdness. He postulated that each interpretant could be one of three kinds and that each of these three kinds could be any of the three modes of being. Thus, he came up with six trichotomies and 28 classes of signs. He later suspected that there were four more trichotomies and hoped he would find only 66 classes, although as many as 59,049 were possible.

[36] Wittgenstein, *Philosophical Investigations*, pp. 31–32.

ing or that meaning is totally subjective. Meaning is inseparable from all thinking and perception; validity is inseparable from reality and truth (though certainly not the same as) and, like them, cannot be determined by any one individual. Even though reality and truth are independent of what you or I may think or believe, meaning is not. That we always have in our rule-controlled use of signs. And we believe in the reality and truth of the meanings we perceive so long as we have no reason to doubt them or can justify them.

What is affirmed is individual freedom to influence the meaning of experience within the realistic, practical constraints of the grounds and language games familiar to us. The notion that is both implicit and explicit in deconstructive theory—that a particular interpretation of a text or a particular worldview is somehow mandated or determined by the "nature of language"—is baseless.

Wallace Stevens said that poetry "is an unofficial view of being" and "is an interdependence of the imagination and reality as equals."[37] Stevens distinguishes between the approach to truth through imagination, as in poetry, and through reason, as in philosophy, but he sees them as equals. Peirce's sign theory supports Stevens in every one of these points. Every perception involves both the imaginative choice and the real laws of sign usage, whether the perception be a Rheme or a Proposition, poetical or philosophical. But there is no text or world for us other than the one we see as a result of the interdependence of choice and necessity as equals. Neither man nor language alone is the measure of things. Things *are* for us through the interdependence of human choices and imaginative or real possibilities offered by cultural language games and forms of life. In legal, historical, scientific, and philosophical matters (signs of fact, class-9 signs, official

[37] Stevens, *The Necessary Angel: Essays on Reality and Imagination* (New York: Vintage Books, 1951), pp. 40, 27.

views), agreement on which rules and grounds count as a valid basis for interpretation is of practical importance. But insofar as our propositions (class-9 signs) are about art (a sign of possibility, a class-8 sign, "an unofficial view of being"), we have no way or pressing need to establish the superiority of one view over another in order to arrive at a norm. Criticism of literature is not so much the effort to establish the superiority of one view over another as it is the effort to share the possibilities of valid interpretation. The interdependence of imagination and reality, private choices and public signs, freedom and necessity, choice and determinism, subjectivity and objectivity—as equals—makes untenable the notions of autonomous imaginations, texts, or language, and of a complete understanding or interpretation.

SEVEN

Theory:
Meaning as a Sign of Reason

> Five minutes of our waking life will hardly pass
> without our making some kind of prediction; and
> in the majority of cases these predictions are ful-
> filled in the event. Yet a prediction is essentially of
> a general nature, and cannot ever be completely ful-
> filled.... If the prediction has a tendency to be ful-
> filled, it must be that future events have a tendency
> to conform to a general rule.... A rule to which
> future events have a tendency to conform is *ipso*
> *facto* an important thing, an important element in
> the happening of those events.
>
> —Charles S. Peirce,
> "The Principles of Phenomenology"

We have shown that according to Peirce's theory of signs a
literary work is a class-8 sign (a Symbolic Rheme or Rhematic
Symbol),[1] which represents "possible" objects, and that the experience of such signs is what we normally call aesthetic experience. Furthermore, we have shown that literary criticism
is a class-9 sign (a Dicent Symbol, or Proposition), which "represents its object in respect to actual existence" and "professes
to be really affected by the actual existent or real law to which
it refers" (2.252). We are now ready to show that literary the-

[1] The reader may find it helpful to review the chart on page 67 and the
diagram on page 74.

ory is a class-10 sign (an Argument), which "represents its Object in its character as Sign." Like the Dicent Symbol, the Argument pretends "to be really affected by the actual existent or real law to which it refers . . . but that is not the principal pretension of the argument" (2.252).

To understand the principal pretension of the argument, a brief review of the symbolic or general nature of all linguistic signs may be helpful because a class-10 sign represents symbols (i.e., conventional signs) in their character as symbols. In defining his second trichotomy (Icon, Index, and Symbol), Peirce says that, unlike the Icon, "which would possess the character that renders it significant, even though its object had no existence," and the Index, "which would, at once, lose the character which makes it a sign if its object were removed, but would not lose that character if there were no interpretant,"

> a *symbol* is a sign which would lose the character that renders it a sign if there were no interpretant. Such is any utterance of speech which signifies what it does only by virtue of its being understood to have that signification. [2.304]

Thus, for Peirce, there are no symbols apart from interpretants, and all linguistic signs are symbols.

> A *Symbol* is a sign which refers to the Object that it denotes by virtue of a law, usually an association of general ideas, which operates to cause the Symbol to be interpreted as referring to that Object. It is thus itself a general type or law, that is, is a Legisign . . . . Not only is it general itself, but the Object to which it refers is of a general nature. Now that which is general has its being in the instances which it will determine. There must, therefore, be existent instances of what the Symbol denotes, although we must here understand by "existent,"

existent in the possibly imaginary universe to which the Symbol refers. [2.249]

According to Peirce, "All words, sentences, books, and other conventional signs are Symbols" (2.292). Thus, a symbol has general meaning (2.293) and "cannot indicate any particular thing; it denotes a kind of thing. Not only that, but it is itself a kind and not a single thing" (2.301). "A symbol is a Representamen whose Representative character consists precisely in its being a rule that will determine its Interpretant" (2.292). Since a symbol is a law, "its Interpretant must be of the same description; and so must be also the complete immediate Object, or meaning" (2.293). A word and its meaning, therefore, are each general rules and "do not differ, unless some special sense is attached to 'meaning'" (2.292). This is essentially Peirce's version of the "linguistic turn." In thought, everything is Thirdness.

Literary art, criticism, and theory are all symbolic, but their difference in character consists precisely in whether they represent their objects as signs of possibility, fact, or reason. A Rhematic Symbol, a Dicent Symbol, and an Argument are different classes of symbols that determine their interpretants and represent their objects according to different modes of meaning. I pointed out in an earlier chapter that literary art, being inseparable from language, partakes of Thirdness (is a Symbol), but creates an interpretant that has the mode of being of Firstness (is a Rheme). Literary theory, like art, is a Symbol, but, unlike art, creates an interpretant that has the mode of being of Thirdness (is an Argument, a sign of reason). It does not represent its objects with respect to fact, as signs of actual existents, as do class-9 signs; it does not represent its objects as aesthetic spectacle, in their characters merely. Rather, it represents its objects as general signs, as conventions, rules, laws.

Theory, like art, has "an admixture of potentiality in it"

(1.420), but it presents us with what is *conceptually* possible, with what is reason-able. Just as Dicent Symbols always involve Firstness as part of their object, Argument involves Rhemes and Dicent Symbols. But, Peirce says, Argument symbolizes Thirdness, which is

> that element of cognition which is neither feeling [Firstness] nor the polar sense [Secondness], is the consciousness of process, and this in the form of the sense of learning, of acquiring of mental growth.
>
> ... This is a kind of consciousness that cannot be immediate, because it covers a time, and that not merely because it continues through every instant of that time, but because it cannot be contracted into an instant. It differs from immediate consciousness, as a melody does from one prolonged note. Neither can the consciousness of the two sides of an instant, of a sudden occurrence, in its individual reality, possibly embrace the consciousness of a process. This is the consciousness that binds our life together. It is the consciousness of synthesis. [1.381]

Peirce repeatedly used the ideas of one-two-three to illustrate the differences between our experiences of Firstness (Rhematic Symbols), Secondness (Dicent Symbols), and Thirdness (Argument). We conceive of "one" as qualitative possibility; "two" incorporates "one" in our consciousness of relation; "three" incorporates "one" and "two" in our consciousness of synthesis or mediation (1.377–382):

> The idea of First is predominant in the ideas of freshness, life, freedom ... measureless variety and multiplicity. ... In the idea of being, Firstness is predominant ... on account of its self-containedness. ... The first is predominant in feeling, as distinct from objective perception, will, and thought. [1.302]

. . . .

The idea of second is predominant in the ideas of causations and of statical force. For cause and effect are two; and statical forces always occur between pairs. . . . In the idea of reality, Secondness is predominant; for the real is that which insists upon forcing its way to recognition as something *other* than the mind's creation. . . . The real is active; we acknowledge it, in calling it the *actual*. [1.325]

. . . .

By the third, I mean the medium or connecting bond between the absolute first and last. The beginning is first, the end second, the middle third. The end is second, the means third. The thread of life is a third; the fate that snips it, its second. A fork in the road is a third, it supposes three ways. . . . Continuity represents Thirdness almost to perfection. Every process comes under that head. . . . Some of the ideas of prominent Thirdness . . . are generality, infinity, continuity, diffusion, growth, and intelligence. [1.337–340]

The Rhematic Symbol and the Argument are similar in that they do not represent their objects to their interpretants with respect to actual existence. But they are quite different in what they do represent. The Rhematic Symbol, as we have seen in Chapter 5, represents its objects, "however complex and heterogeneous" (1.426) as the "merely potential" (1.424), as Firstness.

The immediate present, could we seize it, would have no character but its Firstness. Not that I mean to say that immediate consciousness (a pure fiction, by the way), would be Firstness, but that the *quality* of what we are immediately conscious of, which is no fiction, is Firstness. [1.343]

The Argument represents its objects in their character as signs; it does not represent the character of possible objects or facts, but represents symbols as symbols; that is, it represents thought. The Argument, we may say, is pure Thirdness—Thirdness representing Thirdness. This is its "principal pretension."

It may already have become clear to the reader that what we have just defined as the nature of Argument, of a class-10 sign, is exactly what the structuralists and deconstructionists have defined as the nature of language and literature. In short, they have made all literature into theory of language. They say literature is about itself as literature. They say literature does not primarily represent the ideas of being and possibility, but represents writing writing, symbols symbolizing symbols. Derrida, perhaps because of his focus on the irreducible symbolic nature of language, has made all literature, language, and thought of the character of Peirce's class-10 sign an Argument. Derrida's definition of language as "writing" is an assertion that all language is of the nature of a class-10 sign—symbols representing symbols as symbols. Therefore, much of structural and Derridean theory of language is consistent with Peirce's theory of class-10 signs. It should be clear now why deconstructive theorists cannot distinguish between literature and history or philosophy. It will also become clear why their theories cannot be shown to be true or false.

Since the effort of this book is to get beyond the treatment of meaning in prevailing theory, I have for the most part juxtaposed Derrida and Peirce. However, on many points they are in full agreement. Derrida's conclusions—to the extent that he is reconceiving our relationships to the binary oppositions of (Saussurean) meaning; to the extent he shows that, in a theory of language based on the notion of the dyadic sign, meaning lacks a center, and signs relate within the totally autonomous system of interchangeability permitted by a sort of internal free play—are not much different from those of Peirce. Peirce sounds similar to Derrida in his insistence that meaning is dynamic and takes place in the motion of signs, that it comes to pass in the continuity of consciousness, that it is mediated not by individual signs or objects or complete systems, but by continuity.

Derrida is aware of his agreement with Peirce, and it seems to me that in *Of Grammatology* Derrida could have communicated several of his ideas more simply by using Peirce's definition of a sign. Although Derrida gives only a cursory treatment of Peirce in that work, he does make a few comments that leave one wondering why he did not use Peirce more extensively. In qualifying Saussure's concept of the arbitrary nature of linguistic signs, Derrida says: "In his project of semiotics, Peirce seems to have been more attentive than Saussure to the irreducibility of [the] becoming-unmotivated" of the sign as symbol, or linguistic sign.[2] In this regard, he quotes Peirce approvingly:

> Symbols grow. They come into being by development out of other signs, particularly from icons, or from mixed signs partaking of the nature of icons and symbols. We think only in signs. These mental signs are of mixed nature; the symbol-parts of them are called concepts. If a man makes a new symbol, it is by thoughts involving concepts. So it is only out of symbols that a new symbol can grow. [2.302]

He concludes that Peirce has already done much that his own work sets out to do. Derrida says that

> to make enigmatic what one thinks one understands by the words "proximity," "immediacy," "presence" ... is my final intention in this book. This deconstruction of presence accomplishes itself through the deconstruction

---

[2] Derrida, *Of Grammatology*, trans. Gayatri Spivak (Baltimore: Johns Hopkins University Press, 1974), p. 48.

of consciousness and therefore through the irreducible notion of the trace.[3]

Therefore, it is quite significant that he says "Peirce goes very far in the direction that I have called the de-construction of the transcendental signified [i.e., presence]."[4] Derrida thus recognizes that Peirce's definition of a symbol has within it the destruction of the metaphysics of presence. Derrida's commentary on Peirce's "Principles of Phenomenology" is that it, unlike Husserl's unacceptable phenomenology, is not a theory of things but a theory of signs:

> *[M]anifestation* itself does not reveal a presence, it makes a sign. . . . The so-called "thing itself" is always already a *representamen* shielded from the simplicity of intuitive evidence. The *representamen* functions only by giving rise to an *interpretant* that itself becomes a sign and so on to infinity. The self-identity of the signified conceals itself unceasingly and is always on the move. . . . From the moment that there is meaning there are nothing but signs. We *think only in signs*.[5]

It is within the context of his definition of "trace" that Derrida interjects this commentary on Peirce. The concept of the "trace" remains somewhat enigmatic in *Of Grammatology* because Derrida uses Saussure's concept of a sign to describe what he sees to be a characteristic of signs that cannot be accounted for using Saussure's definition of the sign. One wonders again why Derrida does not use Peirce's theory of signs to get beyond Saussure, particularly when he admits that in specific ways Peirce is superior. Consider, for example, some of Derrida's definitions of "trace":

[3] Ibid., p. 70.
[4] Ibid., p. 49.
[5] Ibid., pp. 49–50.

The trace is in fact the absolute origin of sense in general.
Which amounts to saying once again that there is no absolute
origin of sense in general.

. . . .

That the signified is originarily and essentially . . . trace,
that it is *always already in the position of signifier*, is the
apparently innocent proposition within which the metaphysics of the logos, of presence and consciousness, must
reflect upon writing as its death and its resource.[6]

Peirce, it seems to me, makes it much clearer than Derrida
in what sense all linguistic signs derive their meaning from
"trace," from the character of signs that remains outside of
human consciousness, that cannot be mediated. The preceding chapter shows in some detail that meaning is the dynamic
relation of signs; signs denote previous signs and have meaning in subsequent signs in the continuity of thought. Firstness
and Secondness are for us always already Thirdness, and
Thirdness in thought is always already another Thirdness.
Nothing comes before the mind as an object of thought except
by reference to previous thought. Immediate consciousness is,
by virtue of its immediacy, insusceptible of mediation; therefore, we can never be conscious of it.

While the case could be made that Derrida and Peirce are
not very different in their aims, their strategies are quite different. Derrida's method is to deconstruct, to confuse and con-
found a way of looking at the world that is solely dyadic, binary, by using the very principles it deconstructs—the dyadic
sign and binary oppositions. Deconstruction is not a theory,
but a method for deconstructing theory. Consequently, Derrida almost always finds himself revealing the "negative," the
"preventive," the "difficulties," and speaking of the "bottomless pit," the "abyss," the "hole"—in short, the fundamental
lack that goes all the way back to his conception of the gap in

[6] Ibid., pp. 65, 73.

the dyadic sign where writing writes the play of difference. Even when he wants and claims to be "affirmative," he finds himself able to offer "only, at best, some negative conditions, a 'negative wisdom.' "[7] Peirce's tactic, on the other hand, is to set forth unabashedly a new, comprehensive theory of signs which says that there are no symbols apart from interpretants and no interpretants apart from a ground. If we categorize Peirce and Derrida using Paul Ricoeur's distinction between those who deal lovingly with the symbol (e.g., Rudolf Bultmann, Heidegger, Gadamer) and those who deal with the symbol as a false reality (e.g., Marx, Nietzsche, Freud),[8] Peirce belongs in the former category and Derrida in the latter, not because Derrida does not love language (his style reflects his pleasure in language) but because he shows that, in the diacritical theory of structuralism, meaning is a possible product of a system of signification that is related only to itself.[9] Derrida is dealing with the structurality of structure, and the question of reality has been set aside. Peirce is dealing with the human experience of signs. He says, "The symbol may, with Emerson's sphynx, say to man, Of thine eye I am eyebeam" (2.302, 1.310). Symbols, according to Peirce, enable us to see. A symbol for Peirce, like Thirdness in general, is a medium; a symbol for Derrida, like language in general, is a substitute. Peirce says *meaning is a triadic relation* (a sign stands to somebody for something) *which is inexpressible by means of dyadic relations alone* (1.345). Derrida says language is an autonomous system of dyadic signs independent of sign users,

[7] This passage and all the quoted terms in this paragraph come from Derrida, "The Principle of Reason: The University in the Eyes of its Pupils," *Diacritics* 13 (Fall 1983): 3–20.

[8] See Richard E. Palmer, *Hermeneutics: Interpretation Theory in Schleiermacher, Dilthey, Heidegger, and Gadamer* (Evanston, Ill.: Northwestern University Press, 1969), pp. 43–45.

[9] Anthony Wilden, *The Language of the Self* (Baltimore: Johns Hopkins University Press, 1968), p. 217.

and interpreted meaning is arrived at by stopping, arbitrarily and prematurely, the play of language.

The reason Derrida is accused of finding death, blindness, and illusion everywhere (and one must acknowledge that such terms appear frequently in his texts) is not simply the fact that signifieds are always already signifiers. Peirce does not dwell on these terms, yet he makes a similar statement about signs: in the dynamic nature of signs, representamens ceaselessly give rise to interpretants that become representamens of new signs; and objects can be referred to only by referring to preceding signs. I think one of the reasons Derrida and other deconstructionists are accused of propagating a metaphysics of nihilism is their assumption that all language is of the character of what Peirce calls class-10 signs. From a Peircean perspective, Derrida and the deconstructionists have embraced a partial truth that leads them to infelicitous conclusions. Like Young Goodman Brown in Hawthorne's tale, their theory is at odds with and cannot account for their existential experience. They have concluded that if all language is symbolic, there is nothing in our experience but symbols, and all evidence to the contrary merely shows how blind we are to the supplementary, relational, dynamic character of language; if all symbols are dynamic, then we are loosed into an endless space of symbols detached from any reality other than symbols. Consequently, all acts of closure, of interpretation, must come under suspicion.

Since deconstructionists see language as autonomous and primordial, they make it the "force behind" controlling meaning by the ever opening play of difference. Their theory cannot explain, as Peirce's does, the freedom of human choice that controls meaning as theory. By attributing everything to writing (writing writes), they do not take responsibility for the uncertainty that characterizes the use of symbols to represent symbols. To some, poststructural theory appears to be less a theory for opening meaning than it is a great sacrifice in order to retain a certainty. It sacrifices certainty of meaning for the certainty of differ*a*nce. They say that, in a system of differences, meaning has no center; but, as Anthony Wilden has expressed it, "Derrida's notion of freeplay (which is a center related only to the system) is clearly conceived as something immanent to the structure (like the freeplay in a gear train)."[10]

Peirce recognized that in class-10 signs there is not a necessary choice determining meaning, but unlimited freedom of choice. Such signs do not represent fact, the actual world of action and actuality; rather, they represent reason and what is reasonable.

Just as action requires a peculiar kind of subject matter, one that

> is foreign to mere quality, so law requires a peculiar kind of subject, the thought ... as a peculiar kind of subject foreign to mere individual action. Law, then, is something as remote from both quality and action as these are remote from each other. [1.420]

Since theory, a class-10 sign, represents the general, law, there are no limits on the possible relations of signs except the limits of the human imagination to synthesize, compare, contrast, project, integrate. All that is required for meaning in class-10 signs is "some relation" in thought, that is, law. To the degree that we wish to play with form, with generals, fantasy and daydream have no check. To the degree that we wish to limit the relations of signs to the rules of a particular theory, we will succeed. The deconstructionists, the new creationists, the Marxists, the capitalists, the Jews, the Christians—all are capable of interpreting the facts according to their theories with perfectly good logic. Without a doubt, the definers of class-10 signs control meaning; and, to the degree that they can get

[10] Ibid., p. 218.

their theories accepted as official doctrine, as Thomas Szasz
has said, they control the world.

But when we think of "theory" we normally think of something more serious than fantasy and less political than the will
to power. We think of trying to establish what we might call
"general facts." Of course, there are not such *things* because
"no congeries of actions here and now can ever make a general fact," but we want to find a law or set of laws to which
actual events tend to conform. Peirce says that we do such
serious theorizing all the time:

> Five minutes of our waking life will hardly pass without
> our making some kind of prediction; and in the majority
> of cases these predictions are fulfilled in the event. Yet a
> prediction is essentially of a general nature, and cannot
> be completely fulfilled.... If the prediction has a ten-
> dency to be fulfilled, it must be that future events have a
> tendency to conform to a general rule.... A rule to
> which future events have a tendency to conform is *ipso
> facto* an important thing, an important element in the
> happening of those events. [1.26]

It would be hard to overemphasize the importance of theory to criticism. Theory, meaning in the mode of being of a
class-10 sign, will always "more or less, in the long run, mould
reactions to itself," and "it is only in doing so that its own
being consists" (1.343). This is true both of accepted propositions that mold the conduct of persons into conformity and of
predictions, intentions, anticipations that mold our reactions
to events. I have earlier made the point that Norman Holland
always finds literature to be sublimated fantasies and that
Derrida always finds writing to be writing something other
than what the author intended. Who has not gained a new
insight and then found it confirmed everywhere he or she
looked? That accounts for half the fun of reading philosophy.
I remember Umberto Eco calling for a history of semiotics

and making some suggestions for it. What became clear as he spoke was that, for him, all intellectual history from ancient Greece to the present had become the history of semiotics. Peirce was well aware that meanings or theories in class-10 signs are inexhaustible, that the "steadiness of a hypothesis . . . consists in this, that if our mental manipulation is delicate enough, the hypothesis will resist being changed" (1.322), and that "the brute reactions between things will be moulded to conformity to the form to which the man's mind is itself moulded" (1.343). This, in fact, is the essence of theory and of Thirdness.

Peirce's theory of signs acknowledges that worldviews, theories, and beliefs are generals and, therefore, never fully realized in action or actual events. One is free to choose or reject literary, religious, political, economic, or psychological theory as the expression of one's belief, and it is the nature of these generals to "guide our desires and shape our actions" and perceptions (5.371). They are the mediators, the medium of seeing, of the meaning of life for us. While we are perfectly free to choose, we do not make cavalier choices. We desire the truth; we need to know what to expect of the future; we want our beliefs to be "such as may guide our actions so as to satisfy our desires" (5.375). We seek beliefs we "*think* to be true" because we act on them (5.375). Purposeful action is always the result of a belief. Even though Peirce's pragmaticism places much faith in the "common sense" theories regarding practical matters, he carefully distinguishes between the effect of our beliefs and their truth. When dealing with beliefs about abstract subjects, such as literary theory, which are confirmed not by empirical test but by their reasonableness, we have every reason to be on guard. When we believe something to be true, whether deconstructive literary theory or the existence of God, then that belief to a certain extent determines our actions regardless of whether it really is true or not. And unless we have serious reason to doubt, we will not do so.

Consequently, generals are an indispensable ingredient of reality and stand in an interdependent relation with actual existents to the human mind. Our actions and interpretations involved in "coming to the world" may leave us with a satisfied mind and with pleasing or devastating visions whether our generals are true or not.

If it is now established that theories by their very nature are generals and not fact, are abstract and freely chosen, if it is now clear that theories mold reactions and meanings to themselves, the reader may ask why Peirce's theory of signs is better than Saussure's or Derrida's. Since it has been the effort of this book to answer that question, my answer can serve as the book's conclusion.

Conclusion

First, I have tried to show that Peirce's theory is superior to theories based on the Saussurean sign because it incorporates meaning. The first part of the present book shows that theories based on the dyadic sign cannot give an adequate treatment of meaning. For the most part, my conclusions about the treatment of meaning in structural theory are consistent with, or based on, the conclusions of structural and deconstructive theorists themselves. Peirce's central insight was that meaning is a triadic relation and that "genuine triadic relations can never be built of dyadic relations and of qualities" (1.346). He also demonstrated that "every relation that is *tetradic, pentadic*, or of any greater number of correlates is nothing but a compound of triadic relations" (1.347). Because of the irreducible triadic relation of sign-object-interpretant, purpose (choice) and meaning are involved in every use of signs. Peirce says that all Thirdness, all thought, involves an element of meaning that the other categories lack. "Every genuine triadic relation involves thought or *meaning*" (1.345). Meaning is not reducible to qualities or facts, but is what it is by virtue of imparting qualities to facts in a particular ground or language game.

Second, Peirce's theory is a view from the perspective of human experience, of "an intelligence capable of learning by experience" (2.227). Rather than posit some sort of autonomous system of arbitrary relations independent of sign users, Peirce, without denying the social nature of language, says that "the symbol is connected with its object by virtue of the idea of the symbol-using mind, without which no such connection would exist" (2.299). His theory neither centers nor decenters man; it merely makes mind and language interdependent. Consequently, all meaning (not to be confused with truth) is *for us*.

Third, Peirce's theory incorporates signs of quality and actual existents as well as signs of signs. He does this without making metaphysical assumptions or statements about what is or is not more absolute than what is in thought.[11] He is not even willing to go along with Kant, who says that even though we never transcend the limits of our experience to reach it, the thing-in-itself exists and is real. Peirce's unwavering position throughout his life was that any claim of truth about "any reality more absolute than what is thought in it, is a fiction of metaphysics,"[12] and that "it is perfectly true that we can never attain a knowledge of things as they are. We can only know their human aspect.... [T]hat is all the Universe is for us."[13] Then, however, follows the persistent corollary: "that everything which is present to us is a phenomenal manifestation of ourselves ... does not prevent its being a phenomenon of something without us, just as a rainbow is at once

[11] "Critical Review of Berkeley's Idealism," *Charles S. Peirce: Selected Writings (Values in a Universe of Chance)*, ed. Philip P. Weiner (New York: Dover Publications, 1958), p. 83.

[12] Ibid., p. 82.

[13] 20 May 1911, *Charles S. Peirce's Letters to Lady Welby*, ed. Irwin C. Lieb (New Haven, Conn.: Whitlocks, 1953), p. 43.

a manifestation both of the sun and rain" (5.283). We do have *signs of* quality and fact and have no reason to doubt that they represent real qualities and actual existents at the same time that they represent other signs.

I suspect that Peirce would be critical of poststructural theory for its thoroughgoing formalism, and might accuse it of being metaphysical for relying on a concept about which nothing can be known. Peirce was a pragmatist interested in human living and learning. He had strong contempt for idle philosophy that indulges in ontological metaphysics and produces nothing but "meaningless gibberish" (5.423). The tendency is to think that, because Peirce incorporated signs of feeling and of actual existents into his theory, he had some sort of naïve ontological view. Nothing could be further from the fact. Peirce was definitely concerned with the real, with reality, and with truth; but these are signs, are in the mind, and are "that which, sooner or later, information and reasoning would finally result in, and which [are] therefore independent of the vagaries of me and you" (5.311). Truth and reality are not fictions of metaphysics or unknowable things-in-themselves but are future-oriented concepts that are the "last products" or "final opinions" of the community of minds, and the individual can never perceive them *in toto*. They are general and the normal product of mental action, not the incognizable cause of it.[14] What Peirce has given us is a theory of signs that expresses the inseparability and interdependency of thought and reality, of modes of consciousness and modes of being, of "I" and "that," of the phenomenological and the ontological, of mind and matter.

The fourth reason I find Peirce's theory superior to any of the structuralist theories follows from the third. Peirce's demonstration of the interdependence of imagination and reality, private choices and public signs, freedom and necessity, choice

---

[14] "Critical Review of Berkeley's Idealism," p. 84.

and determinism, subjectivity and objectivity—as equals—shows that many of the problems that have plagued literary studies are artificial problems deriving from misguided efforts to define readers, texts, or language as autonomous and to define correct understanding or interpretation as a completed objective fact. Both the formalist (or "estheticist") and the visionary views of literature that Gerald Graff defines in his book *Literature against Itself* are equally untenable. The prominent literary theories, Graff says, can be arranged on a spectrum between these two views. The formalist view says that literature "is not about reality but about itself."

> [I]t separates the literary work from objective reality, science, and the world of practical, utilitarian communication and defines it as an autonomous, self-sufficient "world" or law unto itself, independent of the external world. It is this formalist notion of the self-sufficient work that usually comes to mind when the term "autonomy" is employed.[15]

The visionary view, according to Graff, says that " 'reality' itself is indistinguishable from literature."

> In this view, "reality" itself possesses order and meaning only insofar as these qualities are imposed on it by the human imagination. . . . [T]he real world does not disappear so much as become a kind of malleable raw material, to be shaped, transformed, and "ordered" by consciousness.[16]

Peirce's theory shows us clearly what Graff seems to recognize, that both extremes are formalist. Graff states, "The visionary view is thus a kind of formalism on the offensive."[17]

[15] Graff, *Literature against Itself: Literary Ideas in Modern Society* (Chicago: University of Chicago Press, 1979), p. 13.
[16] Ibid., p. 14.
[17] Ibid.

Both positions, according to Graff, are strategies to eliminate the referential function of literature. He wants to redraw the lines of combat so that these differing views of poetic autonomy are pitted against theories that do justice to the "reality-centered activity of literature."[18] The issue that Graff wishes to see determined is whether "reality takes its orders from consciousness more than consciousness takes its orders from reality,"[19] whether literature is purely self-referential or mimetic. He enters the fray and acquits himself well on the side of reality and mimesis. Peirce's theory of signs can and should deliver us from such quixotic duels and at the same time grant us the prize for which Graff quests: namely, a rationale for taking art and criticism seriously as unique uses of language through which we rise to an understanding of the world.

Fifth, I find Peirce's theory superior to structuralist theory because Peirce emphasizes that humans are freed, rather than enslaved, by language. After the "final no" to determinate meaning in the thoroughgoing formalism of structuralist theory, which has no center or fixed point, comes the "yes" to meaning in the definition of the sign as triadic. Structural and deconstructive theory's "final no" to meaning is not a denial of meaning, but a denial that people can control it; it is a loss of faith in human action. The "yes" on which the future of the world depends is an acknowledgment, an affirmation that (1) "the human writes, the human thinks,"[20] (2) meaning is that about us of which we are most assured since both a sign and its meaning are general rules and "do not differ" (2.292), and (3) meaning is ultimately grounded not by the rules of rationality, but by human choice.

According to Peirce, language by its nature does not determine whether we see humans to be gods, puppets, prisoners,

---

[18] Ibid., p. 17.

[19] Ibid.

[20] Harold Bloom, *A Map of Misreading* (New York: Oxford University Press, 1975), p. 60.

dupes, vermin, or the lords of creation. Rather, language is the medium that allows us to choose such views. Our world-views, our theories, are purely a matter of our own choosing. We can give reasons for whichever views we like best or find most believable, but Peirce shows us that we must accept the burden of freedom and the responsibility for the meaning of our world. The meaning of events conforms to our theories and beliefs; the future of the world does indeed depend on this "yes."

My belief that human values and choices and language and reality are interdependent is what makes me critical of a theory that can only treat form. Saussure inspired his followers to survey meticulously the island of linguistic signs; whatever they looked at, literature, criticism, or philosophy, they found only formal sign relations. Others, such as Heidegger, Gadamer, and Wittgenstein, chose rather to survey the boundary of the ocean;[21] they saw literature as a manifestation of that about human experience which cannot be put into words, and interpretation as our act of coming to a consciousness of the world through the language games we know and choose. Peirce has provided a theory of signs containing interdependent formal and experiential categories. Peirce would have found simplistic the thinking current today that there is somehow a fixed gulf between signs and reality; that since everything for us is a sign, "reality" is a fiction. "Let us not pretend to doubt in philosophy," he urges, "what we do not doubt in our hearts" (5.265). The core of Peirce's pragmaticism is a refutation of absolute idealism *and* realism and an insistence upon the interdependence of reality *and* thought. He has shown us that the ocean of Firstness flows in a continuous stream through the island of consciousness, which is its human aspect.

[21] This image is borrowed from Paul Engelmann, *Letters from Ludwig Wittgenstein*, p. 97; quoted in Allen Janik and Stephen Toulmin, *Wittgenstein's Vienna* (New York: Simon & Schuster, 1973), p. 191.

Finally, I find Peirce's theory to be more comprehensive than any of the structuralist theories. As I have tried to demonstrate in some detail in these last four chapters, Peirce's theory shows us both the formal and the ontological nature of art, criticism, and theory; it shows us the mode of meaning and the mode of being of each. Moreover, his theory provides a theoretical framework for understanding those existential philosophers who have rejected the positivist attitudes of the objectivist and formalist traditions, and those humanists who think that human values shape meaning and events.

INDEX

aesthetic experience, 73, 76, 78, 79, 82, 86, 92, 98, 102, 122
aesthetics, 72, 87, 98. *See also* aesthetic experience
Argument, 66–67, 74–76, 81, 86, 123–27. *See also* classes of signs
art, 76, 78, 86, 88, 102, 121, 142; literary, 11, 66, 73–90, 124
Atkins, G. Douglas: *Reading Deconstruction, Deconstructive Reading*, 32n, 57n, 58n
Augustine, Saint, 26; *On Christian Doctrine*, 25
Austin, J. L., 44
author, 14, 22, 30, 83, 94, 99, 110–12; death of, 13
autonomy, 50, 86, 91, 97–98, 113, 121, 140; of art, 82; of language, 42, 57, 132, 139; of text, xviii, 83, 139

Baldwin's *Dictionary of Philosophy and Psychology*, 58
Barrett, William: *The Illusion of Technique*, 72n
Barth, John, 49n
Barthelme, Donald, 49n
Barthes, Roland, xii, xvi, 17, 27, 49, 118; on reader/text relation, 20; on "readerly" and "writerly" texts, 21; on structural analysis, 19–20; on textual analysis, 19–20, 26. Works: "The Death of the Author," 13, 14n; *Image, Music, Text*, 13n, 14n; *S/Z*, 19, 21n; "Textual Analysis of a Tale by Edgar Poe," 19n, 20
Beardsley, Monroe, 112; "The Intentional Fallacy," 13
being, xiii, 68, 72, 125, 127; in Heidegger, 80; modes of, 54, 58, 59, 63, 76, 77, 84, 85, 102, 134, 138, 142
belief, 114, 117, 135, 141
Bloom, Harold: *A Map of Misreading*, 140n
Boccaccio, 16, 25
Booth, Wayne, 118
Bultmann, Rudolf, 131

Carlyle, Thomas: *Sartor Resartus*, xii
Cassirer, Ernst, xv, xvi; "Structuralism in Modern Linguistics," xvn
categories, 59, 62–68, 72; relation of, to trichotomies, 66–67
certainty, xiii, 50, 92–94, 96, 113–14, 116, 133
choice, 8, 93–94, 96–97, 120–21, 136. *See also* freedom
classes of signs, 62, 73–75; class-8 sign, 75, 78–79, 82, 86–87, 92, 98, 106, 108, 121–22 (*see also* Rhematic Symbol); class-9 sign, 75, 86, 109, 120–21, 124 (*see also* Di-